Horoscopes of Asia, Australia and the Pacific

Marc Penfield

ISBN: 0-86690-561-8

First Printing: 2006

Cover Design: Jack Cipolla

Published by:
American Federation of Astrologers, Inc.
6535 S. Rural Road
Tempe AZ 85283.

Printed in the United States of America

This book is
dedicated to

LISA MORROW CHRISTIAN
a Sagittarius
with Moon in Aquarius
and
SYLVIE STEINBACH
a double Cancer
with Moon in Aquarius

two dear friends
who were there for me
when I needed them most

Contents

Asia by Region

Eurasia
Armenia, Azerbaijan, Cyprus, Georgia, Russia and Turkey
The Middle East
Bahrain, Iraq, Israel, Jordan, Kuwait, Lebanon, Oman, Qatar, Saudi Arabia, Syria, United Arab Emirates and Yemen
Near East
Afghanistan, Bangladesh, Bhutan, Burma (Myanmar), India, Iran, Kazakstan, Kyrgyzstan, Maldives, Nepal, Pakistan, Sri Lanka, Tajikistan, Turkmenistan, Uzbekistan
Far East and Southeast Asia
Brunei, Cambodia, China, East Timor, Indonesia, Japan, North and South Korea, Laos, Malaysia, Mongolia, Philippines, Singapore, Taiwan, Thailand and Vietnam

Asia by Country

Afghanistan	3
Armenia	7
Azerbaijan	9
Bahrain	11
Bangladesh	12
Bhutan	14
Brunei	16
Burma (Myanmar)	17
Cambodia	19
China	22
Hong Kong	29
Cyprus	31
East Timor	33
Georgia	34
India	36

Bombay	39
Calcutta	40
New Delhi	42
Indonesia	44
Jakarta	46
Iran	48
Iraq	52
Baghdad	55
Israel	57
Tel Aviv	60
Japan	62
Tokyo	66
Hiroshima	69
Kyoto	69
Nagasaki	70
Nagoya	70
Osaka	72
Jordan	73
Kazakstan	75
Korea, North	77
Korea, South	79
Kuwait	82
Kyrgyzstan	84
Laos	85
Lebanon	87
Malaysia	90
Kuala Lumpur	91
Maldives	93
Mongolia	94
Nepal	96
Oman	98
Pakistan	100

Philippines   103
    Manila   105
Qatar   107
Russia   109
Saudi Arabia   113
Singapore (City)   121
    Singapore (Country)   122
Sri Lanka   124
    Colombo   126
Syria   127
Taiwan   130
    Taipei   131
Tajikistan   133
Thailand   135
    Bangkok   137
Turkey   139
    Istanbul   146
Turkmenistan   150
United Arab Emirates   151
Uzbekistan   152
Vietnam   154
Yemen   159

Australia, New Zealand and the Pacific

American Samoa   165
Australia   167
    Adelaide   175
    Alice Springs   176
    Brisbane   178
    Canberra   180
    Darwin   182
    Hobart   183
    Melbourne   185

Perth	187
Sydney	189
Fiji	199
French Polynesia	201
Guam	203
Kiribati	204
Marshall Islands	205
Micronesia	206
Nauru	207
New Caledonia	208
New Zealand	209
Auckland	211
Christchurch	213
Dunedin	215
Wellington	217
Palau	220
Papua New Guinea	221
Port Moresby	222
Samoa	223
Solomon Islands	224
Tonga	225
Tuvalu	226
Vanuatu	227
Bibliography	228

Introduction

As stated in previous books, I began my research into what is called "Mundane Astrology" over three decades ago while working as a cataloguer and bibliographer for an antiquarian bookstore in Hollywood, California. Most of my attention initially concerned the cities and countries of North America and Europe, and after a long trip to Latin America in the late 1970s, material on that region was published in my book *Horoscopes of the Western Hemisphere* (ACS Pubns., San Diego, CA 1984).

Material on Australia and, New Zealand was gleaned after two long trips to those countries and the South Pacific in the early 1980s. Asian data was mainly on the country of Japan where I spent my 40th birthday perusing through files in two university libraries. By the end of the 1980s, brief vignettes illustrating the horoscopes of Asia, Australia and Oceania were published in the *Astrological Monthly Review* which is printed in Sydney, NSW, Australia. Its publisher, Ray Webb, is a friend whom I met on my first trip "down under" and over the next four years, much of the material in this book was first published.

My original idea was to simply reprint those articles, but after careful analysis, I needed to update and add nations which had come into being. Yemen was united in 1990 and five Central Asian nations which were formerly part of the Soviet Union also had to be included. Three trans-Caucasus nations should also be included along with East Timor which shook off its Indonesian yoke.

It's hard to imagine, but at the beginning of the 20th century, only nine countries existed in Asia: Afghanistan, Australia, China, Iran, Japan, Nepal, New Zealand, Oman and Thailand. All the rest were colonies of either European powers or the massive, but ailing, Ottoman Empire. By the time World War II erupted, three more were added to the list: Iraq, North Yemen and Saudi Arabia. Most of the nations in this book were created after World War II, when that conflict severely depleted the coffers of their former masters.

A few countries in this book might not be considered Asian at all. Depending upon which reference book one reads, the former Soviet enclaves of Armenia, Azerbaijan and Georgia could be either European or Asian. Let's call them Eurasian. And then there's Russia, which sits astride two continents, as does Turkey, which is separated continentally by the Bosporus, Sea of Marmara and the Dardanelles. Cyprus is geographically part of Asia, but is now a member of the European Union. If I really wanted to nitpick, I could have placed Egypt into this book as well, as the Sinai peninsula is geographically part of Asia, not Africa.

Some countries in this book will have two horoscopes: one for its original founding, as a monarchy (China and Japan) and another for when a more republican or constitutional government was established (China and Japan). Iraq and Afghanistan, which were originally monarchies, saw their old heads of state deposed in military coups. The chart for Taiwan is the same as for China between 1912 and 1949. The Nationalist government moved its base of operations to this offshore island after the Communists took over the mainland. Yemen has three charts: one for North Yemen, one for South Yemen and one for when these two countries were united. Vietnam has three charts as well: one for Ho Chi Minh's declaration of independence at the end of World War II, one for South Vietnam, which was created after the Geneva peace talks in the mid 1950s, and one for when those two countries were united after three decades of war.

Indonesia presented a problem for me. Technically it was still part of the Netherlands at the end of World War II, when Sukarno proclaimed independence in 1945 (the mother country didn't grant independence until the end of 1949). But after working with the 1949 chart for Indonesia, it just didn't fit nearly as well as did the chart for 1945.

Iraq's chart was also a dilemma. Years ago, I saw a chart with the Sun conjunct the ASC in late Cancer with which I have worked for years. The more usually-shown chart with mid-Leo rising just doesn't hold up using progressions and, transits, so the chart shown in this book differs from what most astrologers generally use for Iraq; but the chart works for me.

Many countries in Asia and Australia and Oceania were granted their freedom by the mother country:

21 nations	from the British Empire
5 nations	from France
4 nations	from the USA
1 nation	from the Netherlands
2 nations	from Australia
1 nation	from New Zealand

Several countries declared their own independence:

8 nations	from the Soviet Union
1 nation	from Pakistan
1 nation	from Indonesia
2 nations	from Japan
2 nations	from China
1 nation	from Malaysia

Ascertaining birth times for countries in this book was made considerably easier thanks to *The New York Times*, *Los Angeles Times* and London's *The Times*. Sometimes, only an approximate time was given—such is the case for Qatar. I had to rectify the charts for Qatar and Nepal based on events which had occurred since their independence.

Freedom often came at midnight, as was the case for most colonies in the British Empire. I also chose to use the midnight time for Israel as that chart for the end of the British Mandate more clearly shows the turbulent events in that country's recent history. Others are free to use the more prevalent time of 4:00 p.m. or 4:37 p.m. time if they desire. Some sources implied that the birth of a country occurred during the day, such as Syria or Lebanon, so I've used a time around noon for those nations.

Noontime births were also used for countries such as Persia, Afghanistan, Oman, Saudi Arabia and Thailand as they were founded as monarchies and a noon birth is often chosen for the foundation of dynasties.

Noontime was also used for modern countries when there was no mention of a time in the local papers. Burma (Myanmar) has a birth time that was chosen by astrologers—they must have done something wrong due to the unfortunate history of that country since its independence from the British Empire. Some birth times were given by astrologers living in those countries.

For cities and countries founded prior to 1800, I have chosen to use Local Apparent Time (LAT) which places the Sun at the Midheaven at noon. If one uses LMT (Local Mean Time) for dates prior to the beginning of the 19th century, their charts could be off by as much as four degrees, especially during the months of November and February. All charts for dates after 1800 are calculated using LMT until those countries adopted Standard Time Zones.

I wish I could have included the charts for every capital city but that was not possible. Some of those cities, like Damascas or Jerusalem, are so old that it would have been a guess at best. Some cities, like Colombo and Kuala Lumpur, are given as their incorporation (or charter) dates because historical records could not be found to ascertain an exact founding date. Some cities were given to me by astrologers living in those countries like the Philippines or Thailand. Hong Kong's birth time was recorded by its founder, while only a month and year were obtained for Tokyo. Charts for cities in Australia were relatively easy to calculate as half of them had accurate birth times while most of the rest had to be rectified from sources which stated "mid-afternoon or shortly after noon." In New Zealand, only Auckland had a birth time; the remainder are approximate.

Asia is a vast continent stretching over 10 time zones. It has 60 percent of the world's population but only 21 percent of its area. Australia, by contrast (an island, a continent and a country) has 6 percent of Earth's landmass but only 0.05 percent of its population. Asia also has 65 percent of the world's refugees, most of them Palestinian or Afghani.

Asia has seven of the world's largest countries in population: China, India, Indonesia, Russia, Pakistan, Bangladesh and Japan. Oceania has three of the least-populated: Tuvalu, Nauru and Palau.

Asia has four of the largest countries in area: Russia, China, India and Kazakstan. In Oceania, Australia ranks number one. Asia and Oceania also have four of the smallest in area: Nauru, Tuvalu, the Maldives and the Marshall Islands.

Five countries are among the world's most dense—Singapore, Bahrain, the Maldives, Bangladesh and Taiwan—and two of its least dense—Mongolia and Australia. Nine of the 15 largest cities are also found in Asia: two in Japan, three in India and one each in China, Bangladesh, Pakistan and Indonesia. Fortunately, China has population control, and India has started family planning centers. Tokyo is the world's largest metropolitan area with more than 25 million people, but it's growing more slowly than Mexico City and Sao Paulo in Latin America, which have yet to conquer over-population and its concomitant poverty and disease.

Finally, I would like to thank Nicholas Campion who wrote the Bible on mundane Astrology, *the Book of World Horoscopes*. This book could not have been written without his vast amount of material not available to us here in America. Nick and I have shared information for several years now, and even though we don't always agree on the chart for a specific nation, his research is of the first order and one which should be applauded for its thoroughness. *Mundane Astrology*, which he wrote with Charles Harvey and Michael Baigent was also a gold-mine of both information and insight. I hope this book will be a nice addition to those books which have done so much to educate those of us who are interested in studying world events, or what some call "mundane" astrology. Believe me, it's anything but mundane!

Mundane Astrology

The Planets

The Sun—Governs the will of the people and their inherent characteristic Rules all political activities and persons in power and authority.

The Moon—Rules the common people, their personality and desire for change. Also has dominion over the basic necessities of life such as food, clothing and shelter.

Mercury—Rules the people's ability and desire to communicate as well as their literary interests and desire for movement and travel.

Venus—Represents the people's desire to make their community more attractive. It governs high society, the arts and culture.

Mars—Governs the energy of the people. It has dominion over manufacturing and industrial concerns. It also rules the police and the military.

Jupiter—Governs the religious and moral principles of a people and their capacity for law and order. It also illustrates the desire to elevate themselves financially or spiritually.

Saturn—Governs conservatism and right-wing elements of society. It also shows the ability to accomplish desired goals and degree of ambition. It also shows the restrictive elements which must be overcome lest ruin and disgrace tarnish the reputation of the community.

Uranus—Has dominion over radical and progressive elements and all left-wing activities. Uranus rules riots, rebellions and all acts which upset the status quo and equilibrium of the community.

Neptune—Governs the ideals of the people as well as their desire to communicate with outsiders. Neptune governs the mass media, all chain stores and places which are franchised. It also governs problems relating to alcoholism, drug addiction and mental diseases.

Pluto—Represents the group effort and degree of cooperation that is to be expected to accomplish a desired goal. Pluto rules transformations, such as urban renewal mergers, foreign alliances and treaties, especially if those relate to finance or trade.

The Houses

First—Represents the people and the first impression one gets when viewing a particular place as well as the disposition, temperament and personality of the people. This house acts as a lens through which the rest of the horoscope is filtered.

Second—Represents the people's attitudes towards material possessions and their sense of values. It shows their potential wealth and assets and all places were earnings and. investments are deposited.

Third—Illustrates the people's ability and desire to communicate. Governs the postal service, the mass media and all forms of transportation and literary interests. Also rules elementary education (K-12).

Fourth—Shows the people's desire for security and ownership of real estate. Governs houses, apartment houses and condos, permanent or transient. Also governs agriculture, farmers and miners. Also has a great deal to do with weather and climate patterns.

Fifth—Shows the people's ability to amuse themselves. Governs theatres, cinemas, gambling halls as well as prostitution. Governs the stock market and other forms of speculation as well as children.

Sixth—Represents the workers of the community or country, especially those in the employ of the government. All civil service workers, police and military come under its jurisdiction. Also governs health concerns.

Seventh—Governs the people's ability to relate to outsiders and their desire to form alliances or treaties. Failure to balance and adjust might result in conflict and could lead to war. Also governs tourism.

Eighth—Shows the debts of the people and their taxation. Also rules insurance companies and credit card firms. This house also illustrates which areas need to be regenerated or destroyed in order for the entire structure to perform at maximum efficiency.

Ninth—Shows the people's desire for law and order. Governs the courts and the church and all forms of higher education such as colleges or universities. All international concerns and commercial interests come under the dominion of the ninth house.

Tenth—Represents the leader of the people, be it their president or prime minister, king or dictator, their mayor or governor. Also shows the people's attitude towards those in power and authority and the general reputation of the community. This house also shows the outcome of elections and referendums.

Eleventh—Represents the friends, allies, supporters and backers of the community. It governs legislators, congressmen, senators and aldermen. Also shows the general philanthropy and bequests to a community.

Twelfth—Illustrates the hidden ills of the community. Hospitals, asylums, jails and prisons as well as those who work in those institutions come under this house's dominion. Those on welfare and support from SSI or unemployment insurance are shown here as well.

Aspects

Aspects can be hard or so ft, what we used to call benefic or malefic. They often indicate specific static conditions (soft) or clarifying obstacles with which one must eventually cope (hard).

Conjunction (0 deg.)—Neither hard nor soft, depending upon the nature of the planets conjoined. This aspect blends varying elements into a single unit. Venus conj Jupiter is easier than Mars conj Saturn, for example.

Semi-square (45 deg.)—Mildly irritating and vexing, like a rash that won't go away because you won't keep from scratching it.

Sextile (60 deg.)—Offers numerous opportunities through social contacts that can be highly beneficial. It's mildly lucky but also energetic.

Square (90 deg.)—Indicates obstacles which must be overcome and the areas of life that need the most improvement and attention. Highly energetic but also frustrating.

Trine (120 deg.)—Indicates a harmonious state of being and potential for luck but in itself is passive and, lacking in energy. Keeps the status quo.

Sesquare (135 deg.)—Indicates frustration and annoyance often with mental anomalies which will require patience and calm.

Inconjunct or Quincunx (150 deg.)—Like mixing oil and vinegar between two forces that will never really mix as they have nothing in common. This is the "fly in the ointment" or "monkey wrench" aspect that requires considerable adjustment or compromise in order to function at all.

Opposition (180 deg.)—Indicates literal opposition in temperament or methodology that exists between two forces which are reluctant to blend that could lead eventually to either cooperation or conflict.

Horoscopes of Asia

Kabul 34N31 69E12 (4:36:48)

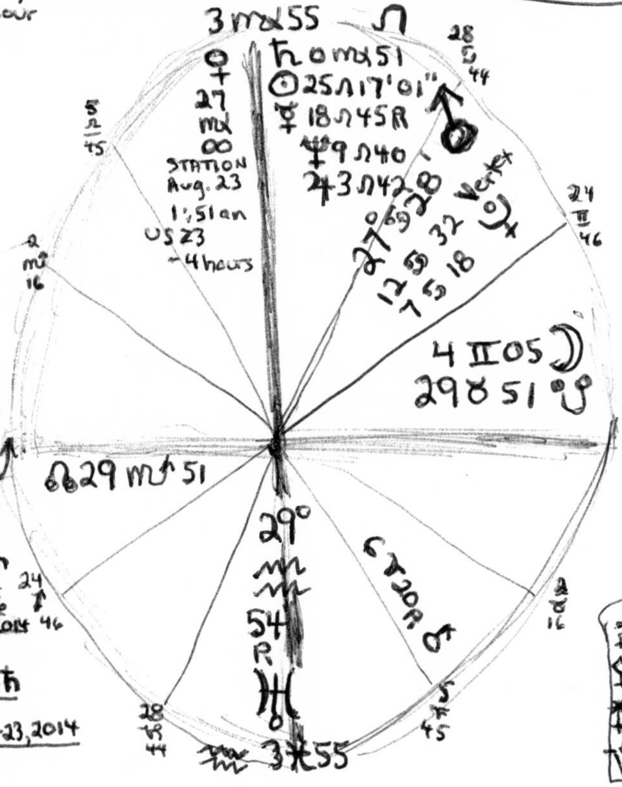

o' day
24 hour   Noon Chart

3 ᠓55

♀
27
m⋏
∞
STATION
Aug. 23
1°51 an
℧♏23
~4 hours

5♏
45

♃ 0 ᠓ 51
☉25 ♌17'01"
☿18 ♌45 R
♀ 9 ♌40
♃ 3 ♌47 28
27 ♋
12 ♋ 5 18
7 5 18
32

♋ 0
69

☊
28
44

Vertex

♂

24
♊
46

4 ♊05 ☽
29 ♉51 ☊

24
♉
33

☊ 29 ᠓ ⵎ 51

24
♏
33

prog.
New Moon
eclipse 24
29 ᠓ 16 ♐
Dec.7, 2014 46

transit ♄
30 ᠓
Dec.15-23, 2014

29°
♒
♒
54
R
♅

♈ 20 R ♆

18
♒
44

᠀ 3 ♓ 55

5
♓
45

2
᠓
16

Declination	
♀	3S49
☿	5N14
MC	10N04
♂	11N26
♅	12S14
♄	12N28
☉	13N05
♆	17N47
ASC	18S54
♇	19N22
♃	19N42
☋	20N07
☽	20N36
☊	21N36
Vertex	22N51

Asteroids			
⚷	4 ♈21 R	11S5	
⚥	19 ♒2 R	11N39	
✶	15 ᠓47	6 N00	
⚴	13 ♐34	10 N48	

2

Afghanistan

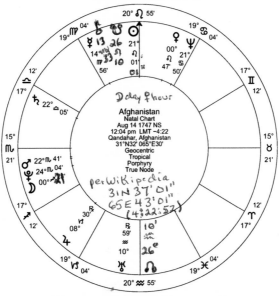

Afghanistan
Natal Chart
Aug 14 1747 NS
12:04 pm LMT -4:22
Qandahar, Afghanistan
31°N32' 065°E30'
Geocentric
Tropical
Porphyry
True Node

per Wikipedia
3 N 37' 01"
65 E 43' 01"
(4:22:52)

August 14, 1747, Noon LAT (12:04 p.m. LMT), Kandahar
Source: Afghan embassy; no time given; noon presumed.

In ancient times, this region was known as Bactria or Khorasan. It has been invaded by Aryans from India, Persians in the 6th century B.C. and by Greeks under Alexander the Great in 330 B.C. By the 18th century, the region was divided between the Persians and the Moghuls from India. Tribes united under Nadir Shah in August 1747 and modern Afghanistan was born. Because Great Britain wanted to protect its investment in India, it invaded the country in 1839, prompting the first Afghan war (MC square Sun conjunct Mars trine Neptune). The war ended three years later (MC conjunct Pluto). Russia also wanted the region in order to gain access to a deep-water port on the Indian Ocean; this sparked the second Afghan war in 1878. Afghanistan signed a peace treaty with Britain in 1921 (MC inconjunct Mercury). The monarchy was overthrown in July 1973 (MC square Jupiter sesquare Sun and Mars; ASC conjunct Neptune).

3

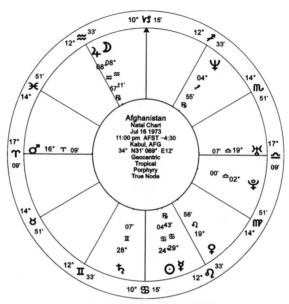

July 16, 1973, 11:00 p.m. ST, Kabul
Source: Los Angeles Times and The New York Times both
state the coup began at 11:00 p.m.

The monarchy was overthrown in a military coup in July 1973. Five years later, pro-Soviet leftists took over (ASC square Sun), which led to the Soviets invading in December 1979 (MC square Mars). After nine years of warfare (of which Osama Bin Laden was a part), the Soviets finally departed in February 1989 (MC opposition Sun; ASC square Moon and Jupiter). More than two million Afghanis died in the conflict and six million people left the country, many to neighboring Pakistan. By 1992, an Islamic government ruled (MC inconjunct Saturn; ASC semisquare Saturn) and in September 1996, the dreaded Taliban took control (MC trine Pluto; ASC square Venus inconjunct Uranus).

Women became second-class citizens, forfeited their careers and were forced to wear the burkha, a garment which concealed their entire bodies except for a narrow slit allowing them to see outside. The Taliban took Islam literally, even more so than the puritanical Wahhabi sect in Saudi Arabia.

4

Beginning in 1998, the U.S. began bombing terrorist camps in Afghanistan run by the Saudi terrorist, Osama Bin Laden, who had worked for the CIA during the years of Soviet oppression. In 1999, the U.N. imposed sanctions on Afghanistan (MC sextile Neptune). When Bin Laden and his group, Al Qaeda, ran two planes into the World Trade Center in New York City, the U.S. invaded this country in October 2001 to get rid of Bin Laden once and for all. He had been allowed to roam at will with the full support of the ruling Taliban (ASC sextile Sun). America has so far failed to capture Bin Laden for he lives in various caves in this mountainous country and may even be living over the border in Pakistan. The Taliban was ousted and a more democratic government was sworn in in June 2002 (MC conjunct Moon and Jupiter).

Afghanistan is a land of 27 million people living in one of the most mountainous and inhospitable regions on earth. It's about the size of the Ukraine or Texas and most of the land is above 4,000 ft. in elevation. The Hindu Kush tower more than 16,000 ft. over the capital of Kabul and tower to more than 23,000 in the east on the border with China. Most of the southern region are deserts. This country is the world's second-largest producer of opium (after Burma), from which heroin is made. Opium is the country's chief export to the outside world.

Looking at the 1747 chart, we clearly see the fighting spirit of the Afghanis. The squares of Mars and Pluto in the first house and the sextile to Saturn in the twelfth indicate a never-say-die situation. The Moon in the ninth trine its ruler, the Moon in Sagittarius in the first, point to the geographical significance of why the British and Russians fought so hard for this region. This resilience continued after the 1973 coup with Mars rising and the tenacious Sun in Cancer in the fourth house. Difficulties with outsiders is shown by Uranus in the seventh, and the religious fervor is shown by the Moon and Jupiter in the tenth.

Kabul

Situated at an elevation of 6,000 feet, Kabul is 120 miles west of the famed Khyber Pass, the gateway to the riches of India. Visited by Alexander the Great in the 4th century B.C., it was made capital of the Moghul Empire in 1504. Partially destroyed by the British during the Afghan War in 1842, it was almost reduced to rubble during the most recent conflict in the 1990s.

Armenia
Haikakan Hanrapetoutioun

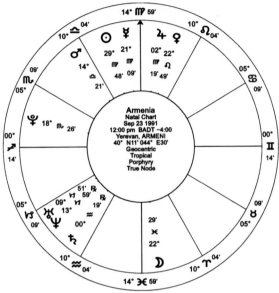

September 23, 1991, noon BGDT (8:00 a.m. GMT), Yerevan
Sources: Book of World Horoscopes by Nick Campion;
no time given; noon presumed.

The first Armenian kingdom was established in 317 B.C., one century before the Greeks arrived in 211 B.C. Romans came in 69 B.C. and ruled Armenia until 232 A.D. The region was partitioned between Persia and Asia Minor in 387 A.D. around the time Armenia became the first country to make Christianity its official state religion. Arab invaders came in 653 A.D. but had little overall influence in changing the status quo. Direct rule from the Byzantine capital in Constantinople began in 1046, two centuries before the Mongols laid waste to the region.

Russian occupation began in 1828 and lasted until first declared its independence in May 1918. But freedom was short-lived due to the arrival of the Bolsheviks in December 1920. Armenia joined

7

the USSR in December 1922 as part of the Trans-Caucasus Republic and became a separate republic 14 years later.

With the break-up of the Soviet Union, Armenia again declared its independence in September 1991. Shortly thereafter, fighting broke out with neighboring Azerbaijan over the disputed region of Nagorno-Karabakh (progressed MC sesquare Saturn; progressed ASC semisquare Mars). In October 1999, the Prime Minister was shot by terrorists during an attempted coup in Parliament (progressed Sun semisquare Venus; progressed MC opposition Moon; transiting Neptune inconjunct Jupiter). Since independence, over one-third of Armenia's people have emigrated due to a pervasive energy shortage. Many went to America.

Armenia is situated in the center of the Trans-Caucasus region between the Caspian and Black Seas at the juncture of Europe and Asia. Most of the country is more than 3,000 feet in elevation; the highest point is Mt. Aragats (elev. 13,500 ft.). The population of 3.5 million lives in an area the size of Belgium or Maryland. The capital is Yerevan.

August 30, 1991, Noon BGT (9:00 a.m. GMT), Baku
Source: Los Angeles Times says 9:00 a.m. GMT

King Atropates established an independent state during the 4th century in a region known in ancient times as Scythia. Turkish armies overran the area during the 11th century to be followed by the Persians and Mongols two centuries later. Russia conquered the region in 1813, but its southern part was ceded to neighboring Iran 15 years later. A railroad to the Black Sea was completed in 1883, enabling Baku to become the world's leading oil producer of the late 19th century.

In May 1918, an. independent republic was formed, but freedom was fleeting as the Soviet army entered two years later. Azerbaijan became a charter member of the USSR in December 1922 as part of the Trans-Caucasus Republic. In December 1936, it became a separate republic. In 1988, fighting with Armenia began over the ethnic enclave of Nagorno-Karabakh which continues to this day.

Azerbaijan again declared its independence from the dying Soviet Union on August 30, 1991. World attention was soon focused on oil pollution in the Caspian Sea and this country soon became famous for being the world's most ecologically-devastated region. In November 1995, a new Constitution expanded the powers of the President (progressed ASC sextile Saturn) and in January 2001, Azerbaijan was admitted to the Council of Europe.

Azerbaijan is located on the shores of the Caspian Sea. More than 40 percent of the country is lowlands and 10 percent lies below sea level. The Greater and Lesser Caucasus Mountains are separated by the fertile valleys of the Kura and Arak rivers. Almost eight million people live in an area the size of Maine or Hungary. The capital is Baku.

Bahrain
Mamlakat al-Bahrayn

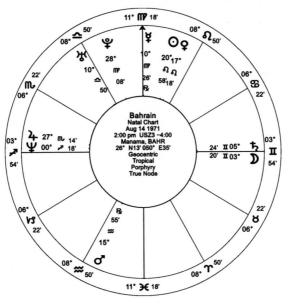

August 14, 1971, 2:00 p.m., Manama
Source: Kuwaiti radio broadcast.

The Arabs invaded and brought Islam in the 7th century. The Portuguese claimed the region from 1521 until 1602. The Khalifa dynasty has ruled since 1783. Bahrain became a British Protectorate in 1861 and was granted freedom and independence in 1971. Parliament was abolished in 1975, however, so this is no more a democracy than is neighboring Saudi Arabia (MC inconjunct Mars).

Oil was discovered in 1932 but most of its reserves are now gone. International banking has taken over as the chief source of income.

Bahrain is slightly smaller than New York City with a population of fewer than one million. The country consists of the island of Bahrain and 34 smaller islands.

Bangladesh

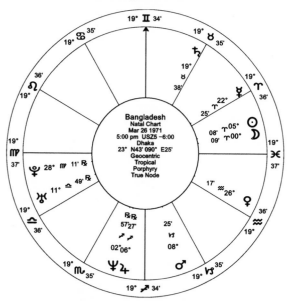

March 26, 1971, 5:00 p.m., Dhaka
Source: The Times of London states 5:00 p.m.

Turkish Moslems conquered this region then known as East Bengal during the 12th century. It became part of the vast Moghul Empire in 1526 and was incorporated into the British Empire of India in November 1858. British rule ended in August 1947 and this region was then known as East Pakistan. The capital of Karachi was more than 1,000 miles to the west on the other side of India.

In November 1970, a devastating cyclone killed thousands and left untold millions homeless and flood waters inundated much of this region. The call for independence erupted in March 1971, when Pakistani troops arrested the President and a civil war erupted. Over the next nine months, nine million Pakistanis fled to neighboring India. India finally stepped into the conflict in December 1971 and a treaty was signed between India and Pakistan granting this region's freedom, December 16, 1971 at 4:31 p.m. Indian troops left the following March.

A coup in October 1977 caused martial law to be instituted which was lifted 18 months later (Sun opposition Uranus; ASC inconjunct Venus). Two years later, the President was shot in another coup, the Constitution was suspended and another round of martial law ensued (MC square Pluto; ASC conjunct Pluto). In May 1981, another president was shot and his successor was ousted in a coup one year later. An Islamic Republic was created in 1988, one year after another devastating cyclone tore through the region (MC inconjunct Jupiter).

Looking at Bangladesh's chart, we note the Balsamic Moon in the seventh. Even though both luminaries trine Jupiter and Neptune, they also square Mars in the fourth house of the land, and Mars governs the eighth house of death. Mercury, ruler of the ASC and MC, opposes Pluto in the first. Clearly this country must come to terms with Mother Nature and the catastrophes she brings. The Sun also semi-squares Saturn pointing to its limited economy and the Sun opposing Uranus and square Mars also point to illnesses which occur frequently in this part of the world.

Bangladesh is probably the poorest country in Asia and definitely the most crowded. More than 130 million people live in an area the size of England or Florida. The poverty rate keeps growing at such a rate that the government is powerless to control the increase. Bangladesh is basically a low flood plain between the deltas of the Ganges and Brahmaputra rivers. It's as if the U.S. had housed millions of people on the swampy lowlands of the Mississippi delta in Louisiana. Rainfall is very heavy and the entire region is susceptible to inundations during the monsoon season. The capital is Dhaka. which was founded in 1608.

Bhutan
Druk Yul

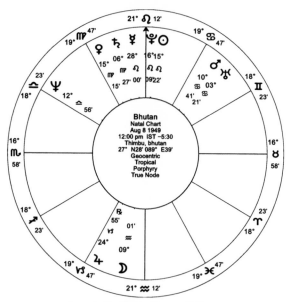

August 8, 1949, Noon, Thimpu
Source: Indian Embassy; no time known.

Prior to 1630 when a Tibetan named Dupka Lama became the first Raja, little is known about this region cradled by the Himalayas. For the next two centuries, internal strife was rampant until the British annexed the southern part of Bhutan in 1865. By 1910, Britain had assumed control of foreign relations some three years after a hereditary monarchy was formed.

In August 1949, a treaty was signed with Britain which returned lands previously taken, and on paper at least, Bhutan was finally independent. In 1959, the border with Tibet was closed after China annexed that region (ASC sextile Jupiter sesquare Mars). In recent years, the journey to India has been made easier with the completion of a highway which cuts down the travel time from six days to only five hours or so.

14

Situated on the southern slopes of the Himalayas, the highest mountain range on earth, southern Bhutan is composed of thick, dense forests on which most of the half-million people live. Bhutan is the size of New Hampshire and Vermont combined.

Brunei
Negara Brunei Darussalam

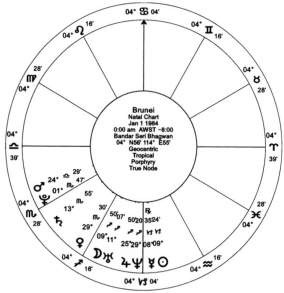

January 1, 1984, 12:00 a.m., Bandar Seri Baghwan
Source: Los Angeles Times says midnight.

Before the arrival of the Portuguese in the 16th century, Brunei occupied a large portion of the island of Borneo. Over the next few centuries, the Dutch and British carved up Borneo so that by 1888, when the British established a Protectorate, only a small fraction remained. Oil was discovered in 1929 and remains the main source of income. In 1971, Brunei became self-governing and achieved independence in 1984. During 1997, the Asian financial crisis caused severe hardships on the Sultan's finances. He was once reputed to be the wealthiest person alive and he lives in the largest palace ever constructed in modern times.

Brunei is completely surrounded by Malaysia on the island of Borneo. Its 350,000 citizens live in an area the size of Delaware or twice the size of Luxembourg.

16

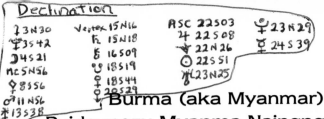

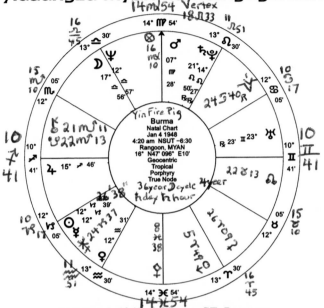

Burma (aka Myanmar)
Pyidaungzu Myanma Naingngandaw

Burma
Natal Chart
Jan 4 1948
4:20 am NSUT –6:30
Rangoon, MYAN
16° N47' 096° E10'
Geocentric
Tropical
Porphyry
True Node

January 4, 1948, 4:20 a.m. ST, Rangoon
Sources: Embassy of Burma; Nicholas Campion.

About the 11th century, a Buddhist monarchy was established. Two centuries later, the Mongols invaded in 1287. Now part of the Chinese state of Shans, the invaders were driven out in 1546. During the 19th century, three wars broke out against the British who ruled Burma since 1885 as part of their Indian Empire. Burma became self-governing in 1937.

Burma suffered heavy casualties during the Japanese occupation from 1941 until 1945. Britain finally granted independence in January 1948 and the time was chosen by Hindu astrologers, possibly to have Jupiter rising with the Sun and Mercury trining the Midheaven.

On threat of a civil war in 1962, a military dictatorship was formed (MC semisquare Pluto; ASC opposition Uranus). Over the next 25 years, Burma would drive out all Indians and Chinese and socialism was instituted. Burma isolated itself from its neighbors and turned its face inward, shown natally by Venus in the third house opposing Pluto in the ninth. Serious riots erupted in 1988, ending Ne Win's dictatorship. Burma also changed its name to Myanmar at this time (ASC inconjunct Pluto).

Sagittarius rises pointing to the strong religious bent of the Burmese people. The opposition of its ruler, Jupiter, to Uranus in the seventh, which rules the third house of neighbors, might well explain why Burma has so isolated itself from the outside world. The Sun and Mercury in the exclusive sign of Capricorn also square Neptune and inconjunct Pluto.

Burma, surrounded by mountains on three sides, is a nation of 42 million people in an area the size of France. Its capital, Rangoon (or Yangon), was founded centuries ago and was renovated in 1753. It was heavily bombed by the Japanese during their occupation in World War II.

Burma is the world's leading producer of opium, which is converted into heroin. This narcotic is the chief export as Burma is part of the "Golden Triangle" in southeast Asia.

Rangoon (Yangon)

Rangoon was developed as a port in the 18th century and became the capital of Lower Burma in 1852 and capital of Burma by 1886. Its most famous structure is the Shwe Dagon pagoda which dominates the city's skyline at 328 feet and is covered with thousands of sheets of gold. Rangoon's fortunes have dwindled since the British left in 1948.

The capital was moved to Pyinmana in late 2005 on the advice of astrologers who warned that the government would fall if the capital were not moved. Planning for this move began in 2000, but for the present, most embassies will remain in Yangon.

Cambodia
Preah Reach Ana Pak Kampuchea

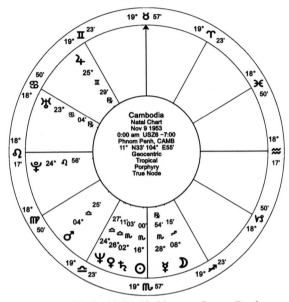

November 9, 1953, 12:00 a.m., Pnom Penh
Source: Bibliotheque Nationale in Paris says midnight.

During the 1st century AD, the Kingdom of Funan was founded which in turn was conquered by the Khmers in 802. This vast empire lasted for six centuries. Its capital, Angkor Wat, is one of the main tourist attractions in southeast Asia. The French made this region a Protectorate in 1863, and Cambodia became part of Indo-China in 1887. During World War II, France lost hold on this region and granted autonomy in 1946. Even though France granted this area independence in 1953, it wasn't until the Geneva Accords were signed in July 1954 that France truly recognized the independence of Cambodia.

Beginning in 1963, Prince Sihanouk allowed Vietnam to construct military bases along its border (MC square Mars/Neptune; ASC sextile Venus square Mercury). Soon after, relations with the

19

U.S. were broken due to aerial bombings during the Vietnam War in 1965 (MC inconjunct Saturn). In October 1970, Lon Nol seized power and changed the country's name to the Khmer Republic (MC opp Moon semisquare Uranus), and the monarchy was abolished. Over the next five years, a civil war erupted between Lon Nol's troops and the Khmer Rouge.

The Communists took over in April 1975 and changed the country's name to Kampuchea (MC sesquare Venus; ASC semisquare Neptune). The new regime proceeded to evacuate people from the cities and moved them into the countryside to endure years of torture and genocide under Pol Pot. By the time Vietnam invaded Cambodia in 1978 (MC inconjunct Sun) more than one million had perished or were executed. The capital was captured and Lon Nol fled into the jungle where he carried on his guerrilla warfare to regain power. Thousands fled to neighboring Thailand where they lived in refugee camps. By 1985, Vietnamese forces had overrun most of the Khmer Rouge bases. On the verge of another civil war, Prince Sihanouk left Cambodia shortly before a coup by troops loyal to Hun Sen took over (MC square Mars; ASC conjunct Mars). In April 1998, the madman Pol Pot died. In 1994, the monarchy was restored (MC sesquare Sun; ASC semisquare Sun).

Many of the problems this country has had to endure could be shown by that rising Pluto sextile Jupiter and Neptune. All hopes and expectations of good fortune carried a price that was extremely steep in terms of lives lost during the 1970s. Uranus squares Neptune as well, pointing to outsiders trying to dominate the original regime. Uranus rules foreigners and Neptune governs the 8th house of death. Note also the Sun in Scorpio in square aspect to the ASC degree as well as its square to the ruler, Pluto.

More than 75 percent of Cambodia is forested and 13 million people live in an area the size of Missouri, or twice the size of Portugal. The capital, Pnom Penh, was founded in 1371 and has been abandoned many times since its founding.

Phnom Penh

Situated on the Mekong river, Phnom Penh has been the capital of Cambodia since 1434. During the Pol Pot regime in 1975, the city was depopulated from nearly two million to a mere 23,000 five years later. The Vietnamese occupied the city from December 1978 to 1989.

China
Zhonghua Remnin Gongheguo

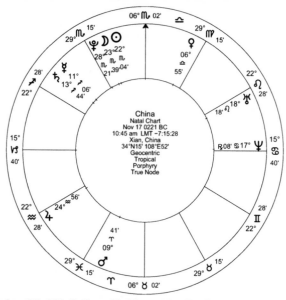

November 17, 221 B.C. at 11:00 a.m. LAT, Xian (10:45 a.m. LMT)
Source: Chinese Emperor by Jean Levi states China was founded
by Emperor Chin on the first day of the tenth Moon. The actual
New Moon occurred at 8:17 a.m. LMT, but since this chart is
for the foundation of a dynasty as well as a country, I've rectified
it to a time about 11:00 a.m.

The first chapter of Chinese history is lost to antiquity. The first
dynasty, the Hsia, is largely mythical and recorded history doesn't
begin until the Shang dynasty (1766-1123 B.C.). During the Ghou
dynasty the great philosophers Confucius and Lao-Tza were born.
In 221 B.C., China was unified by the Emperor Chin for whom the
entire region was named. The Great Wall of China was constructed shortly afterwards. During the Han dynasty, paper was invented and the arts and sciences flourished. Until 589 A.D., China
was beset with internal strife and often invaded by tribes from the
Asian steppes. During the T'ang dynasty, printing, mechanical

clocks and gunpowder were invented.

By the time Marco Polo visited China (Cathay) in the late 13th century, this country was the most technologically-advanced nation on earth. Ruled by Kublai Khan, the first Emperor of the Yuan or Mongol dynasty, he was the grandson of Genghis Khan, the Mongol warrior who conquered lands at the doorstep of Europe. The Mongols ruled until 1368, when the Ming dynasty ushered in the Golden Age of China. In 1644, Manchus invaded from the north and founded a dynasty that would rule China until its collapse in the early 20th century.

The final years of Manchu rule were humiliating to China as foreign powers divided up the country for their own benefit. The British came in 1839, peddling their opium which the Chinese tried to destroy. This provoked the Opium War of 1839, which lasted for three years (MC square Mars semisquare Sun/Moon; ASC conjunct Venus semisquare Sun). In 1842, the Treaty of Nanking was signed which granted trading concessions to foreign powers (MC inconjunct Mercury opposition Jupiter/Pluto; ASC opposition Mars sextile Mercury sesquare Jupiter). More concessions were granted by the Treaty of Tianjin in 1858 (MC trine Pluto sesquare Mercury/Saturn; ASC trine Jupiter).

Japan began flexing its military and naval might with the Sino-Japanese War of 1894-95 (MC square Sun/Moon; ASC square Uranus trine Neptune). China lost and its humiliation fulminated until June 1900, when the rebels lashed out at foreigners. It was called the Boxer Rebellion and outsiders were held inside their embassy compounds for 55 days until troops arrived to quell the revolt (MC square Pluto). A revolt that began in October 1911 brought down the Manchu dynasty (ASC conjunct Pluto), and on January 1, 1912, a Republic was founded with Sun Yat-Sen as its leader.

Sun Yat-Sen's rule lasted only 43 days as he had no political experience. He fled to Japan where he tried to obtain support for his ambitions (MC semisquare Venus). Civil war broke out in 1917 (ASC square Neptune) and by 1922, China received financial aid from the Soviet Union (MC semisquare Jupiter). That same year,

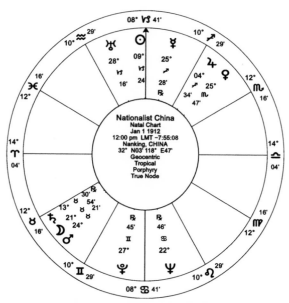

January 1, 1912, noon, Nanking
Source: Memoirs of Sun Yat-Sen

the Nationalists (or Kuomintang) and the Communists joined forces. But by 1927, Chiang Kai-shek turned on the Communists as he conducted the Northern Expedition whereby he hoped to rid China of dissidents and revolutionaries.

China was invaded by the Japanese in September 1931, and a puppet state was set up in Manchuria to house Japan's ever-increasing population (ASC conjunct Saturn). Chiang's fight against the Communists forced Mao Tse-tung on his Long March in 1934 of more than 6,000 miles (ASC conjunct Mars/Saturn). Chiang himself was kidnapped in December 1936 in an attempt to reunite the Nationalists and Communists (MC sextile Jupiter; ASC conjunct Moon). Both sides decided to cooperate when the Japanese invaded eastern China in July 1937 and the capital was moved further inland to Chungking (ASC sextile Neptune). Japanese occupation lasted until August 1945, when Japan returned to China territories previously taken like Taiwan and Korea (MC square Saturn sesquare Pluto). After the war, civil war erupted and the Com-

24

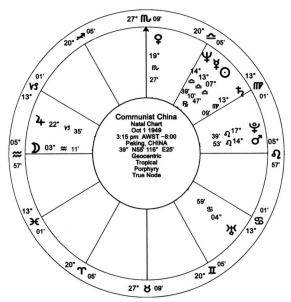

October 1, 1949, 3:15 p.m., Peking
Source: CBS radio broadcast; astrologer, Charles E. O. Carter

munists had the Nationalists on the run. Peking was captured in January 1949, and on October 1, 1949, Mao proclaimed the People's Republic of China from a balcony on Tiananmen Square (ASC opposition Jupiter semisquare Neptune). The Nationalist government under Chiang Kai-shek fled to Taiwan two months later.

The Nationalist government fled to Taiwan in December 1949, two months after the Communist takeover. China aided the North Koreans in their conflict against the South Koreans and U.N. troops by November 1950 (MC semisquare Mercury; ASC trine Sun). China also began a massive land reform program and a five-year plan to kick-start the economy. During the next four years, more than one million were executed during Mao's purge to rid his country of negative elements (MC sextile Moon; ASC trine Mercury inconjunct Saturn).

The Great Leap Forward was a noble exercise that began in

25

1958, but it ended in failure two years later after massive famine (MC sextile Sun; ASC opposition Pluto sesquare Uranus). By 1958, relations with the Soviet Union had turned sour as the USSR refused to share its nuclear technology with China. A revolt in Tibet erupted in 1959, which forced the Dalai Lama to flee to India (MC sextile Sun; ASC square Venus). A border war with India erupted the following year. The next great program, called the Cultural Revolution, began in 1965 (MC sextile Mercury square Saturn) and resulted in numerous purges and relocation of millions of Chinese, especially the young to the cities. It ended, mercilessly, in 1968 (ASC trine Uranus).

With the United States pulling a few strings, China was admitted into the United Nations in October 1971 and Taiwan was forced out (MC semisquare Moon). Four months later, U.S. President Nixon visited Mao in Peking and steps were taken which would lead to U.S. recognition of China almost a decade later. Mao died in September 1976 and Deng Xiao-ping took over (ASC semisquare Moon inconjunct Pluto). Leftists were placed under arrest and efforts were made to reform certain policies. In 1981, China took its first census in years and to no one's surprise, it was home to more than one billion individuals.

Students advocating democracy began to stage demonstrations in Peking in May 1989 after the death of one of their leaders. Violence escalated by early June 1989 and tanks began to fire on the students (MC square Sun; ASC opposition Mercury inconjunct Saturn). It was a spectacle seen around the world on TV and an event the Chinese were reprimanded for harshly, not just by the media, but politically as well.

During the 1990s, China made extensive economic improvements and in a few years had become the world's fourth-largest economy. A modified capitalist system was allowed and several free-trade zones were founded. Deng Xiao-ping died in February 1997 and Jiang Zemin took the helm of the largest nation on Earth. Four months later, Britain ceded Hong Kong back to China (MC square Neptune inconjunct Mars). True to its Communist origins, China cracked down on the religious cult, Falun Gong, in July

1999 and the sect was banned (MC inconjunct Pluto). At this time, the progressed Sun of China was also conjunct its natal Midheaven.

China is the third-largest nation on earth in area. More than two-thirds of the country is mountainous and only five percent is fit for agriculture. Rolling hills in the north separate China from Mongolia, while the Himalayas separate China from the Indian subcontinent. Geographically, China is almost a square, through which traverse the Yellow and Yangtze rivers, always prone to devastating floods. Today, China is an economic powerhouse, manufacturing practically anything one can imagine and cheaper than anyone else can due to cheap labor, lax work rules and scant pollution controls.

Canton (Guangzhou)

Situated on the Pearl River, Canton was already a major maritime center during the Han dynasty more than 2,000 years ago. Portuguese traders arrived in 1514 and British merchants came a century later. The first Opium War erupted here in 1839 when the British tried to force China to buy this narcotic. The Chinese resisted for three years but eventually lost. Canton is the port from which most of the Chinese in America departed their homeland and the base for the spectacular cuisine they brought.

Nanking (Nanjing)

Situated on the Yangtze river 155 miles west of Shanghai, it was the capital of Chiang Kai-shek's Nationalist government from 1928 until 1937 when the Japanese invaded and killed thousands of people, in an orgy of brutality and savage annihilation.

Peking (Beijing)

Lying on the North China plain 65 miles from the port of Tientsin. The Khitians made it their capital in the 10th century A.D. and three centuries later, Kublai Khan established Peking as his capital. During the 15th century, the third Ming Emperor laid out the present city with the Imperial City within which was the Forbid-

27

den City, China's most popular tourist sight. Peking has been the capital of China since then with the exception of 1928-1949 when the Nationalist government resided in Nanking.

The center of Peking is Tiananmen Square (100 acres) home to the Great Hall of the People and the Memorial Hall which houses the remains of Chairman Mao Tse-tung, founder of the People's Republic in 1949. The Great Wall of China is situated 50 miles north of the city and on the way there one passes the tombs of 13 Ming emperors and the summer palace of the last Empress of China.

Shanghai

China's most populous and cosmopolitan city sits on the Huangpo River some 20 miles from the East China Sea. Besides being China's main seaport, it's also the country's largest manufacturing center which includes iron and steel, shipbuilding, chemicals and textiles. The city grew rapidly at the end of the 19th century when foreign powers were granted special privileges and lived in special enclaves. The heart of the city was the Bund, a promenade along the river with skyscrapers and posh hotels. Shanghai's skyline is the most impressive in the country and possible in the entire Orient, with the exception of Hong Kong.

Tientsin (Tianjin)

Founded as a garrison town, it grew during the 19th century as a port for Peking which was 65 miles away. Until 1949, when the Communists took over, it had been popular with foreigners who enjoyed special rights of residence. Today, Tientsin is a major communications center and oil refiner.

Wuhan (Hankow)

Situated on the Yangtze river, Wuhan is actually three cities: Wuchang, Hankow and Hanyang. It was here that the revolt began in late 1911 which led to the overthrow of the Manchu dynasty and the establishment of Nationalist China on New Years Day 1912.

28

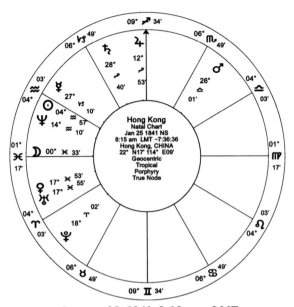

January 25, 1841, 8:15 a.m. LMT
Source: Capt. Ellicott's journal says 8:15 a.m.

Hong Kong

Hong Kong was founded by the British during the Opium Wars. From its original settlement (Victoria), it gained Kowloon in Oct. 1860 (progressed MC sextile Moon; ASC semisquare Neptune). The New Territories were leased for 99 years in July 1898.

Civil war erupted in China in July 1937 (progressed MC conjunct Venus and Uranus; progressed ASC trine Mars opposition Saturn) and in December 1941, the Japanese occupied the region (progressed MC semisquare Sun; progressed ASC trine Moon). Civil government was restored in 1946.

With the emergence of Communist China under Mao-tse-tung in October 1949, thousands of refugees began to pour into Hong Kong (progressed MC square Saturn). This was the impetus to make this region one of the world's banking and industrial powerhouses over the next five decades. Emigration again soared in June 1989, after the Tiananmen Square massacre in Peking leading to

29

even more overcrowding. Hong Kong became a part of China in July 1997 (progressed MC square Neptune; progressed ASC opposition Neptune). China agreed to limit its influence on the region both politically and economically down the road in the future.

Hong Kong has 389 square miles lying at the mouth of the Pearl River about 90 miles south of Canton (Guangzhou). Its population is about seven million. Besides tourism, the chief industries are textiles, apparel, electronics and shipbuilding.

Hong Kong's neighbor, Macao, also reverted to Chinese control on December 20, 1999. This six square mile enclave was founded by the Portuguese in 1557 and in recent years had become a gambling resort.

Cyprus

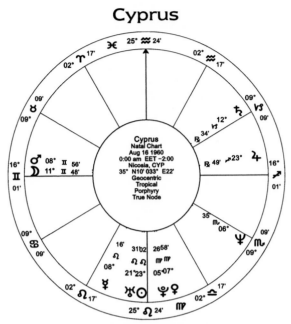

August 16, 1960, 12:00 a.m., Nicosia
Source: New York Times says midnight

First settled more than 10,000 years ago, by 2000 B.C. it was the center of Mycenean culture from Greece. One thousand years later, the Phoenicians arrived from the Levant. Cyprus was annexed to the Roman Empire in 58 B.C. and to the Byzantine Empire in 395 A.D. The Knights Templar proclaimed Cyprus a Crusader state in the late 12th century. Ceded to Venice in 1489, it fell to the Ottoman Turks in 1571. Britain gained control in 1878 and it was made a Crown Colony in 1925. Cyprus became a detention camp for emigrants wishing to move to Palestine after World War II and riots broke out in 1954 as Cypriot Greeks wished to unite with their mother country.

After independence, Archbishop Makarios became its first leader. U.N. peacekeeping forces were called here in 1964 to quell riots (progressed Sun square Saturn); a decade later in July 1974, Makarios was ousted and within days Turkey invaded the northern part of Cyprus (progressed MC square Mars). Makarios returned to power in December 1974. Turkey proclaimed the partition of Cyprus in June 1975, but the occupied territory didn't emerge as a separate country until November 15, 1983 (progressed ASC semisquare Uranus sextile Pluto trine Neptune). Northern Cyprus is not recognized by any country but Turkey. Cyprus joined the European Union in May 2004 despite the fact that it is technically a divided country (progressed MC sextile Mars trine Mercury inconjunct Venus; progressed ASC semisquare Venus and Pluto).

Cyprus is the third-largest island in the Mediterranean Sea, situated off the southern coast of Turkey. Two mountain ranges border a wide central plain—the coastline is 403 miles long. The highest point it Mt. Olympus (elev. 6,401 ft.) This island is 78 percent Greek and Orthodox and 18 percent Turkish and Moslem. Cyprus has 3,572 square miles, one-third the size of Belgium.

East Timor
Republika Democratika Timor-Leste

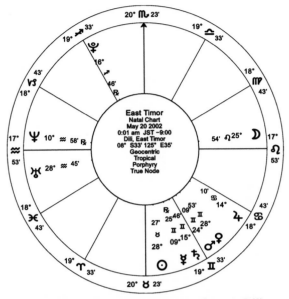

May 20, 2002, 12:01 a.m. (zone 9 east), Dili
Source: BBC. Ceremony was delayed by 23 minutes.

The Portuguese settled this region in 1520 and formally ruled from 1860. After the political coup in Portugal in 1975, the Portuguese pulled out and Indonesia took over. A referendum in 1999 sparked revolts by the civilian militia and East Timor reverted to control under the United Nations. Independence was finally achieved in May 2002.

East Timor has about one million people, most of whom are Christian. It has an area of 5640 square miles, about the size of Connecticut or half the size of Albania.

Georgia
Sakartvelo Respublica

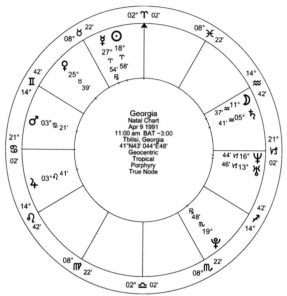

April 9, 1991, Noon BGDT, Tbilisi
Source: Book of World Horoscopes by Campion. No time
mentioned; noon presumed.

To the ancient Greeks, this region was known as Colchis, the land of the Golden Fleece. Christianity arrived in the 5th century A.D. and the Arabs brought Islam three centuries later. In 1236, Georgia was conquered by the Mongols.

In 1801, Georgia asked Russia for protection from the Turks and Persians, thus beginning two centuries of occupation. In May 1918, Georgia declared its independence from Russia but it soon became a German protectorate until World War I ended six months later. Britain then assumed the mandate until July 1920. Bolshevik occupation arrived in February 1921 and by the end of December 1922, Georgia had become a charter member of the Soviet Union in the Trans-Caucasian Republic. In December 1936,

Georgia became its own SSR as did Armenia and Azerbaijan.

Independence from the Soviet Union was declared April 9, 1991 but it refused to join the CIS later that year. The President of Georgia fled the country in January 1992 after trying to establish a dictatorship. Five months later, the district of Abkhazia declared its independence (MC square Mars trine Jupiter). In August 1995, Shevardnadze was wounded by a car bomb on his way to sign a new Constitution (MC sextile Saturn). In February 1998, he again escaped an attempt to assassinate him (MC semisquare Venus).

Situated in the Trans-Caucasus region on the border between Europe and Asia, Georgia lies on the eastern shore of the Black Sea. It has Europe's highest point, Mt. Elbrus (18,510 feet) on the border with Russia. Georgia is a land of turbulent rivers, dense forests, deep ravines and fertile valleys. About five million people live in an area the size of the Netherlands and Belgium combined or the size of West Virginia in the U.S. The capital is Tbilisi, founded in 455 A.D.

India
Bharat

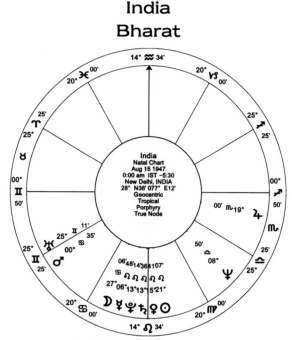

August 15, 1947, 12:00 a.m. IST, New Delhi
Sources: New York Times, The Times of London and Freedom at
Midnight by Collins state midnight.

The Indus River valley is home to one of the world's oldest civilizations which sprang up around 3000 B.C. Aryans migrating from Persia conquered the region about 1500 B.C. Northwestern India was conquered by Alexander the Great in 327 B.C., but the emerging Maurya Empire drove them out soon afterwards. Asoka the Great unified northern India in 273 B.C. and made Buddhism the state religion. During the 8th century, Arabs brought Islam to this sub-continent and laid the groundwork for the Moghul Empire which would rule India from 1526 until 1857.

The first Europeans in India were the Portuguese who landed in 1498 and founded the colonies of Goa and Pondicherry. Beginning in 1609, the British East India Co. began to form settlements.

The power of the Rajas was limited in 1835 and in 1857, the Indian sepoys mutinied against the British. To quell further disturbances, the East India Co. had to give up their rulership and the Indian Empire was founded on November 11, 1858 in Allahabad.

The independence movement began in 1919 with Mohandas K. Gandhi as its leader. He fought for a Constitution which was promulgated in 1935. Independence came in August 1947 when the last Viceroy, Lord Mountbatten, resigned and the region was divided into three countries: India, Pakistan and Burma. Civil war erupted immediately between the Hindus and Moslems who slaughtered each other, especially in Bengal (MC opposition Venus sesquare Mars). Gandhi was shot in New Delhi in January 1948. Nehru, the first Prime Minister, had to deal with over two million refugees fleeing from one country to another. India was proclaimed a Republic in January 1950 and left the British Commonwealth.

Ever since independence, the regions of Jammu and Kashmir were claimed by India and Pakistan. The Chinese invaded those regions in 1962 (MC trine Mars; ASC sextile Venus) making matters even worse. Two years later, Nehru died (ASC inconjunct Jupiter). Two years later, Nehru's daughter, Indira Gandhi, became Prime Minister. A revolution broke out in East Pakistan in March 1971 whereby Indian troops were sent into the region to terminate the revolt. India signed a peace treaty with Pakistan in December 1971 granting freedom to East Pakistan which would henceforth be known as Bangladesh (MC inconjunct Neptune).

In 1974, India became the first third-world country to detonate an atomic bomb (ASC conjunct Uranus). The following year, India annexed the small kingdom of Sikkim in the Himalayas and Indira Gandhi suspended individual liberties for the next two years to quell threats of an internal revolt (MC inconjunct Saturn and Pluto; ASC semisquare Saturn and Pluto.

Gandhi herself was assassinated in October 1984 (MC inconjunct Sun; ASC sesquare Jupiter). Less than two months later, India's worst industrial accident occurred at Bhopal when gas escaping from a chemical plant, owned by Union Carbide, exploded and sent more than 2,500 to their deaths.

Indira Gandhi's son, Rajiv, succeeded her as Prime Minister and was himself removed from office in 1989 on corruption charges (MC square Uranus). Two years later in May 1991, Rajiv was assassinated (MC trine Moon sesquare Saturn and Pluto; ASC square Neptune).

In March 1993, India's biggest wave of criminal violence erupted after Hindu militants destroyed a Moslem mosque. Bombs went off in Bombay and Calcutta, more than 300 were killed (MC square Mars sesquare Venus).

In July 1997, India's first lowest-caste president, K. R. Narayanan, took office and six weeks later Mother Teresa passed away (MC sesquare Jupiter).

In 2002, more than one million troops (75 percent Indian) were mobilized on the Kashmir frontier (MC opposition Neptune; ASC trine Jupiter) in hopes of desensitizing tensions between Pakistan. The world held its breath as both of these nations harbor nuclear weapons.

India has Gemini rising which points to a country of great divisions and multiple races, religions, languages and customs. Gemini's ruler, Mercury, occupies the sign of Leo, the region of kings, potentates and maharajahs who amassed untold wealth during their time in power. The stellium in Leo could indicate the undercurrent of violence which periodically erupts as the planet of peace and mediation, Venus, conjuncts Saturn and Pluto and squares Jupiter and semi-squares Mars. Of course, neighboring Pakistan has the same chart. The Mars/Uranus conjunction straddling the second house make it imperative that India establish a strong industrial base in order to feed her ever-growing population, also shown by Jupiter (ruling the eighth house) squaring the MC. The trine of the Moon to Jupiter illustrates the strong religious feelings of the Indian people, be they of Hindu, Moslem, Buddhist or Sikh persuasions which required India to be split into two nations at the time of independence.

India is home to one billion people, at present the second-largest country on earth, surpassed only by China which has a lower birthrate. It's also the second-largest nation in Asia (after China) with 1.25 million square miles–one-third the size of China and about the same size as Argentina. India is a fascinating country with magnificent scenery, majestic palaces but incredible poverty. More than 1,500 languages are spoken with 1,650 dialects (Gemini rising). India is geologically and geographically a sub-continent, a region which for eons has been pushing its way north through time to create the highest mountains on the planet, the Himalayas, whose highest peak is Mt. Everest (elev. 29,025 ft.). Below the Himalayas lie the fertile plains of the Ganges and Brahmaputra rivers and in the center lies the Deccan plateau. The climate ranges from sub-Arctic to tropical, and the region of Assam holds the world's record for the most rainfall in one year. Over 25 percent is forested but the northwest is largely desert.

Bombay Mumbai

First settled thousands of years ago, this city was named after the Hindu goddess, Bomba Mumba, a consort of Shiva. Its name means "good harbor." The Kohls settled Elephant Island around the beginning of the 1st century A.D. calling their city Ruri. The mainland wasn't settled until 1312. Bombay was conquered by the Moslems in 1348 and besieged by the Portuguese in 1507, who took formal possession in 1534. After the marriage of King Charles II of England to Catherine of Braganza, Bombay was given as a dowry to the newly-wedded king. England took formal possession in 1668, four years later it became a headquarters for the East India Company as the MC was conjunct Jupiter. The following year as the MC opposed Mars, the Dutch were finally driven out. In 1853, India's first railroad reached Bombay from the Deccan (progressed MC opposition Mercury) and four years later, the University of Bombay was founded (MC opposition Jupiter). After the opening of the Suez Canal in 1869 (ASC conjunct Saturn square Jupiter), Bombay soon became the industrial, commercial and financial heart of the sub-continent.

Bombay is situated on an island fourteen miles long and only five miles wide. Its one of the most densely packed cities on earth

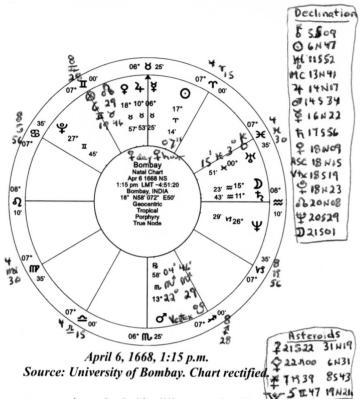

Declination
☊ 5S09
☉ 6N47
♅ 11S52
MC 13N41
♃ 14N17
♂ 14S34
☿ 16N22
♄ 17S56
♀ 18N09
ASC 18N15
Vtx 18S19
⊕ 18N23
☊ 20N08
♇ 20S29
☽ 21S01

Asteroids
♀ 21S22   31N19
♀ 22N00   6N31
⚹ 7N39   8S43
⚶ 5II47   19N24

April 6, 1668, 1:15 p.m.
Source: University of Bombay. Chart rectified.

and home to over six and a half million people. The architecture ranges from exotic oriental to the Victorian monoliths, including the city's symbol, the Gateway of India.

Calcutta

Calcutta was founded in 1699 by Job Charmock for the British East India Company on the site of a village called Kalikata. Six years later, Ft. William was erected to secure the region (ASC sextile Mars). Free trade was established in 1717 increasing the city's fortunes (ASC square Sun and Mercury).

The most famous event in the history of Calcutta occurred in June 1756 when the Nawab of Bengal attacked the city causing most of its inhabitants to flee (MC square Pluto, ASC sextile Saturn and Neptune). Some 146 were taken prisoner and placed into what became known as "The Dark Hole of Calcutta" where only 23 were taken out next day. Admiral Clive took the city in 1757

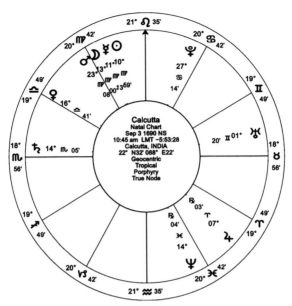

September 3, 1690, 10:45 a.m.
Source: National Library of India. Chart rectified.

and constructed a mint (MC semi-square Moon).

Clive moved the city down-river and the old fort was abandoned, in 1722, Calcutta became the capitol of Bengal and later of British India (MC conjunct Saturn trine Neptune). The government moved to Delhi in 1912 (ASC sextile Moon) after completion of the new capital city. In 1926, riots broke out (ASC sextile Mars) followed four years later by even more devastation, (ASC conjunct Pluto). In late 1942, the Japanese bombed the port (ASC semisquare Mars) but never captured the city. Riots broke out again in 1946, followed by the influx of millions of refugees when India was given her freedom the following year (MC sesquare Mars). After East Bengal revolted against their Pakistani overlords in 1971, more refugees streamed into the region creating further problems and straining facilities to breaking point (MC conjunct Uranus, ASC semi-square Venus). In 1977, the Marxists took over the city's government, and things began to look up for the first time in decades (MC sextile Jupiter).

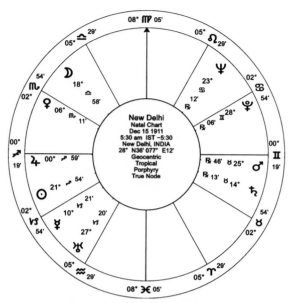

December 15, 1911, 5:30 a.m.
Source: National Library of India for the date and time.

Located at the east bank of the Hooghly, Calcutta is a city that has to be seen to be believed. Untold misery, squalor and filth line most of its streets and beggars are everywhere. Note that Saturn rises indicating hardship and Scorpio rises on the ASC pointing to the fact that living here is often a lesson in sheer survival. Eight universities are located here in a city where more than 75 percent are illiterate (Mercury opposition Neptune semisquare Pluto). The once-booming port is nearly deserted and the airport has been relegated to a second class airfield. One- third of Calcutta lives in slums (Neptune in fourth) with little or no electricity or indoor plumbing. Thousands more live in the streets, many dying there on the sidewalks. It's a crowded and frustrating place, but one of much dynamism despite the overwhelming odds.

New Delhi

The first settlement in the region occurred about 1400 B.C. along the banks of the Jumna, some 100 miles south of the Himalayas. The present city of Delhi was founded in 993 A.D. and named after Raja Dbilu. In 1192 it fell to the Arabs, who made it their capital. After Tamerlane conquered Delhi in 1398, the capital was temporarily moved to Agra until the Moghuls came to power in 1526. The British arrived in 1803 but made Calcutta, not Delhi, their capital in 1858. In 1911, King George V of England laid the foundations for the eighth city on this site and the following year, the government moved here from Calcutta.

The most famous site in Delhi is the Red Fort. The wide avenues of the new city contrast sharply with the narrow alleys of the old oriental city. The combined area of the two cities is 109 square miles and home to 3.5 million people, only 10 percent of whom live in the new sector.

Hyderabad

Capital of the state of Andhra Pradesh (300 miles northwest of Madras), it was founded in 1589. This city with a seven-mile long wall with 13 gates was the former capital of the Nizam of Hyderabad, one of the world's richest men when India was founded.

Madras

Capital of Tamil Nadu state, Madras is the main eastcoast port of India. Founded by the British in 1639 as Ft. St. George and it was chartered in 1688. It rivalled Calcutta as the most important town in British India during its early years. Madras is famous for its textiles and also automobile plants and a center for motion pictures.

Bangalore

Situated 200 miles west of Madras on a high plateau, Bangalore was once popular with British retirees because of its cooler climate. Now the city is a center for aircraft and electronic firms as well as computer companies, hence its nickname "the silicon valley of India."

43

Indonesia
Republik Indonesia

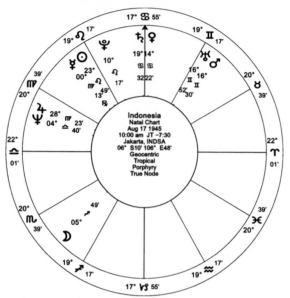

August 17, 1945 at 10:00 a.m., Jakarta
Source: Sukarno's autobiography says 10:00 a.m.

Around 1000 B.C., Malays arrived from the mainland and set-tled this vast archipelago. During the 12th century, the Arabs ar-rived and turned this nation into the world's largest Moslem coun-try. The Portuguese arrived in Malacca in 1511 and stayed until 1623 when they were ousted by the Dutch. By 1750, the island of Java had been subdued and soon the rest of the region fell. The in-dependence movement began in 1927 with Sukarno leading the movement. Two days after the Japanese surrender in August 1945, Sukarno formally proclaimed the independence of Indonesia.

The Netherlands granted independence in late December 1949 and a Republic was formed. Sukarno ruled as virtual dictator after 1957 (MC sextile Jupiter) and quelled a Communist coup in 1965 which killed more than 300,000 before the reign of terror ended

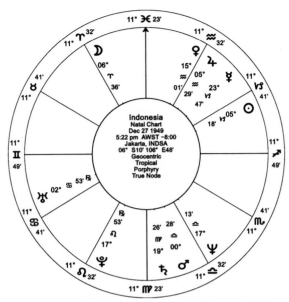

December 27, 1949, 5:22 p.m. (9:22 a.m. GMT)
Source: New York Times says 10:22 a.m. in Amsterdam

(ASC trine Venus semisquare Jupiter). General Suharto took the reins of power in 1968 (MC conjunct Pluto; ASC inconjunct Mars and Uranus). Civil war broke out in Timor in 1975 when the Portuguese pulled out (MC sextile Mars and Uranus; ASC square Sun).

The usual practice of burning the fields and forests produced massive forest fires and tremendous haze in late summer of 1997 whereby most of Southeast Asia was the victim. Suharto resigned in May 1998 (ASC inconjunct Venus). Riots in Molucca erupted in 1999 between Christians and Moslems and more than 2,500 were killed. A deep undersea earthquake in late December 2004 off Sumatra produced a massive tsunami that damaged and destroyed many shoreline communities, not only in Indonesia but also in Thailand and Sri Lanka (MC square Mars and Uranus).

Indonesia is a land of contrasts, geographically, politically and philosophically. The Venus/Saturn conjunction at the Midheaven clearly points to the two strong leaders (Sukamo and Suharto) which ruled this country for the first five decades of its modern history. Saturn, ruler of the fourth house, sesquares the Moon, ruler of the Midheaven, could well indicate the high degree of volcanic activity in this country which falls within the Pacific Ring of Fire. The most famous volcano, Krakatoa, erupted with brute force in August 1883 and sent up so much dust and ash that sunsets glowed red for months after the eruption. A tsunami killed thousands and it was reputed to have been heard thousands of miles away.

Indonesia consists of more than 13,600 islands straddling the Equator for more than 3,300 miles. Java is the most densely-populated region on earth. Besides Java, other main islands of interests are Bali, Sumatra, Borneo, Celebes and Timor. Indonesia also occupies the western half of New Guinea which they call New Irian. Indonesia is home to 210 million people of which over 30 percent are Moslem in an area three times the size of Texas or the Ukraine.

Jakarta

Founded in Sunda Kelapa in 1527, the city grew slowly until the Dutch anived in 1614 and renamed it Batavia (ASC sesquare Sun square Mars). They razed the old city four years later (ASC sextile Moon) and dedicated their new city on March 4, 1621 (MC trine Venus). During the 17th century, Batavia was the centre of Dutch commerce in the East Indies until the huge earthquake of 1699 leveled the town (MC square Mars). During the following century, the Dutch neglected Batavia due to malaria epidemics which erupted periodically.

Vigilantes roamed the city in 1740, trying to quell the crime wave which had blossomed against Dutch rule (MC square Jupiter). A modern harbor was completed east of the city in 1877 (MC semi-square Jupiter) thus increasing the city's fortunes. The Japanese occupied Batavia at the end of 1941 (MC square Pluto inconjunct Mars) but four years later they were ousted. In 1949, Batavia's name was changed to Djakarta (MC opposition Moon) now spelled without the first letter of its new name. Massive flooding in 1977 caused over two-thirds of the city to be inundated

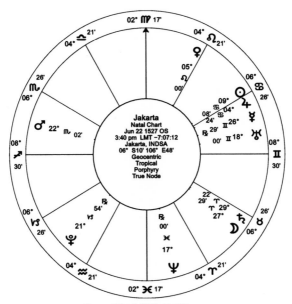

June 22, 1527, 3:40 p.m.
Source: Embassy of Indonesia. Chart rectified.

(ASC sesquare Sun) due to its scant elevation above the sea.

Built on the banks of the Chilliwong river, Jakarta bears many reminders of its Dutch past. Canals are everywhere and the architecture in the old sector is anything but oriental. Most of Jakarta is quite modem and housing projects continue to obliterate what remained of the gardens the Dutch left behind. Jakarta contains 235 square miles and is home to nine million people.

Iran
Jomhuriye Eslamiye Iran

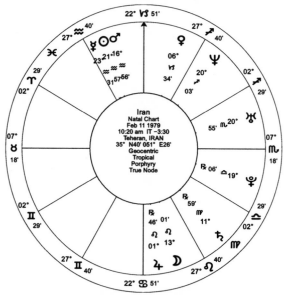

February 11, 1979, 10:20 a.m. ST, Teheran
Source: New York Times says 10:20 a.m.

Nearly four millenia ago, this region then known as Persia was invaded by the Aryans from central Asia and India. Cyrus the Great founded the Persian Empire when he conquered Babylon in late October 539 B.C. Succeeding monarchs like Darius and Xerxes ruled an empire which ranged from Libya to Pakistan. It was a region that worshiped Zoroaster (or Zarathustra) who believed in fire-worship. Alexander the Great conquered Persia in 331 B.C. on his way to India. For the next five centuries, Persia was ruled by the Seleucidae from Syria, a colony of Greece.

Arabs invaded in 651 and replaced Zoroastrianism with the Moslem faith. Genghis Khan ravaged the land in 1220 and Tamerlane came rampaging in 1370. This was the time of the poet Omar Khayyam and the birth of Sufism. Native Persian rule re-

48

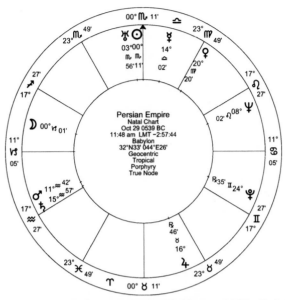

October 29, 539 B.C., noon LAT (11:48 a.m. LMT), Babylon;
no time given; noon presumed.
Source: Babylon by A. T. Olmstead.

turned in 1502 and lasted until 1736. Nadir Shah conquered, neighboring Afghanistan in 1747 but the Persian Empire began to disintegrate in 1813 when portions were lost to Russia.

Modern Iranian history begins in October 1906 when the Shah opened parliament (Majlis) and two months later signed the Constitution. The Pahlavi dynasty came to power in 1925 and ten years later, Persia changed its name to Iran. Because of Shah Reza Pahlavi's pro-German sympathies, he was forced to resign and his son, Mohamed Reza Pahlavi, became shah in 1941. When Mossadegh became Prime Minister in 1951, he seized the Anglo-Iranian Oil Co., which prompted a British blockade which was broken with the aid of the CIA.

The Shah formed a one-party state in 1975 and opponents who resisted his reforms were jailed or tortured by the Savak. Civil unrest began in 1978 and culminated with the Shah's departure on a "vacation" in January 1979. Two weeks later, the Ayatollah Kohmeini returned from exile in France to seize power. His troops took over the government on February 11, 1979.

On November 4, 1979, some 90 hostages were taken inside the American Embassy; they weren't released until January 1981, on the day Ronald Reagan took office. War with neighboring Iraq broke out in the fall of 1980 (MC sesquare Saturn; ASC trine Saturn) over the waterway at the mouth of the Tigris and Euphrates rivers. The conflict lasted for eight years with disastrous results for both sides. Thousands were killed or crippled and in the end, there was no real victor when it ended in 1988 (MC opposition Moon; ASC opposition Uranus inconjunct Neptune and Pluto sesquare Venus). The Ayatollah Kohmeini died in June 1989. After the first Gulf War in 1991, more than one million Kurds from Iraq flooded into Iran (MC semi-square Neptune; ASC square Mercury). In 1997, a moderate Shiite cleric, Khatami, was elected but clashes continued with hard-liners and religious conservatives (MC inconjunct Saturn; ASC sextile Moon).

In many respects, Iran is an attempt to return to the Middle Ages due to the overly strict policies of its Islamic government which wields the Koran like a sabre. Western ideas, music and clothing are frowned upon in this theocracy.

Iran is a land of more than 65 million people living in an area twice the size of France and Germany combined. Only two-thirds are Iranian, the rest being Kurdish or Turkish. The main language is Farsi. Despite being an Islamic nation, Iran is not an Arabic country. Most of Iran lies on a plateau surrounded by high mountains. Large salt deserts are found in the south near the Persian Gulf, while the Caspian Sea forms much of its northern border.

Teheran

Situated at the foot of the Elburz Mtns. which rise to more than 18,000 feet just east of the city, Teheran is 60 miles south of the Caspian Sea. It's been the capital of Persia/Iran only since 1794. The heart of the city was redesigned by Reza Shah in the decade prior to World War II to look more like a western city by demolishing the old walls and creating broad, straight boulevards. Main points of interest include the Pahlavi Palace where the Shah resided until his departure in 1979 and the Majlis, or Parliament Building.

Iraq
Al-Jumhuriyah Al-Iraqiyah

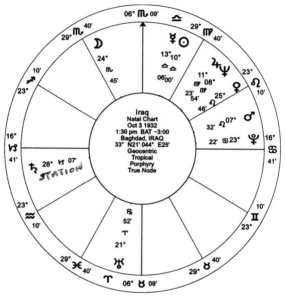

October 3, 1932, 1:30 p.m. BGT, Baghdad
Source: League of Nations records state the vote was taken at 11:30
a.m. (10:30 a.m. GMT) in Geneva. Chart has been relocated.

Iraq, home to some of the world's oldest civilizations when it was known as Mesopotamia gave birth to the Sumer, Chaldean, Assyrian and Babylonian empires. It was a rich land lying between the Tigris and Euphrates rivers. Conquered by the Persians in 539 B.C. under Cyrus the Great and by the Greeks under Alexander the Great in 333 B.C.

With the coming of the Arabs in the 7th century A.D., a Caliphate was founded in Baghdad which soon became the most opulent city in the region. Ottoman Turks took over in 1534 and held the reins for the next four centuries.

Iraq was made a British mandate by the League of Nations in 1920; 12 years later, they granted independence. A military coup

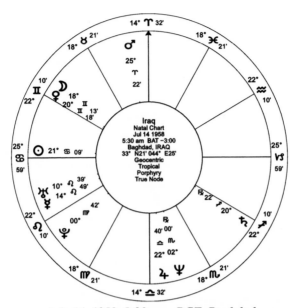

July 14, 1958, 5:30 a.m. BGT, Baghdad
Source: Baghdad radio broadcast, and AFA. Another time floating
around uses 7:00 a.m. (see Introduction).

in July 1958 ousted the monarchy and a republic was formed (progressed Sun conjunct MC).

Five years later, another coup made Iraq a one-party state (progressed Sun square Mars; MC sextile Moon and Venus trine Saturn). Saddam Hussein began his dictatorial rule in July 1979 (progressed Sun conjunct Uranus; MC semi-square Moon; ASC conjunct Uranus).

In 1980, a long and bitter was with neighboring Iran began. When the conflict ended in 1988, both sides had amassed huge casualties and no clear victor emerged (progressed Sun sextile Venus trine Saturn; MC square Mercury; ASC sextile Moon). Iraq invaded tiny Kuwait in August 1990 which it deemed part of its territory (progressed Sun sextile Jupiter; ASC sextile Venus trine Saturn). Five months later, however, a U.S. led coalition invaded Iraq and within six weeks, Kuwait was liberated but with most of its oilfields in flames. A strict no-fly zone was established in northern and southern Iraq: one to protect the Kurds whom Hussein had been harassing for years and the other to protect Kuwait. Sanctions were also imposed on Iraqi oil and revenues plummeted.

After September 2001, when the U.S. War on Terror began, Hussein's days were numbered. President Bush was convinced that Saddam was stockpiling "weapons of mass destruction" even though U.N. inspectors could find no such arsenals. But the U.S. invaded Iraq anyway in March 2003 and Hussein fled Baghdad. He was found hiding in a small bunker near his hometown in December 2003 (ASC conjunct Pluto). Meanwhile, a new government more favorable to U.S. interests in the region was sworn-in at the end of June 2004 but repeated attacks by insurgents are threatening the stability of the new political process. Continued attacks at U.S. and allied troops are a daily occurrence and even civilians, journalists and emissaries are not immune from harm. Iraq could well become America's new Vietnam, a conflict that goes on for years with no harmonious resolution and where the bad guys might just win in the end. Iraq has also become a training ground for terrorists spreading their "holy war" against western nations.

Viewing the chart for Iraq, the first thing one sees is the cardinal T-square between the Sun/ASC, Mars and Jupiter. This clearly points to the overly aggressive stance of this country since the emergence of Saddam Hussein. The Sun square Mars indicates impulsiveness, impatience and general forcefulness especially militarily and the Sun square Jupiter points to recklessness and willingness to take chances, not to mention a certain self-righteousness. Mars opposition Jupiter is also a gambler's aspect where the chase is often more exciting and also where there might be an undercurrent of religious zeal. With Mars and Jupiter square the Sun in the twelfth house, Iraq often has been brought down a peg or two and likes to play the role of victim while it's in the doghouse of public opinion.

Note also the Moon-Venus opposition Saturn. One indicates possible tact and diplomacy and salesmanship, but in opposition to the ruler of karma points to an inferiority complex where the world

54

community is concerned. I've seen hundreds of natal charts with the inner planets opposite Saturn where those individuals tried very hard to be loved, acknowledged for their brains or their personality, but somehow they felt they always came up short in the end. Iraq, I suppose, would like to be admired but it tries to hard to overcome the strictures of the past with resultant paranoia, inferiority and depression.

The Mercury-Uranus conjunction in the first house indicates the erratic, stubborn and often perverse thought processes and communication that seems to surround this country. Despite the broad-minded reputation of Uranus, in national charts this aspect often indicates that leaders never listen to their advisors or follow common sense as they're always going against the grain. Pluto in the second house of wealth sextile Neptune points to Iraq's oil reserves, reputed to be some of the largest in the world, but the ruler of the second house (the Sun) inconjunct Saturn clearly shows the difficulty in getting those resources to market.

Baghdad

Twelve years after the Caliphate was established in 750 A.D., Al-Mansur decided to erect a new city on the site of an older town also called Baghdad. The round city of Mansur, or the City of Peace, stood on the west bank of the Tigris river, but no traces of it remain today. The walled city was 3,000 yards wide and pierced by four gates. No bazaars were permitted inside its walls so the commercial district grew up outside.

The Golden Age of Baghdad occurred during the reign of Harun-al-Rashid, who made this city a center for learning and art. After Harun's death, a civil war broke out and the Caliphs abandoned Baghdad (MC conjunct Jupiter; ASC square Pluto). In 1095, a new wall was built around the eastern perimeter (MC trine Mars; ASC opposition Pluto). More than 800,000 inhabitants of Baghdad had been killed during the invasion. In 1401, Tamerlane sacked the city and the Persians invaded, in 1508 (MC sextile Sun; ASC sesquare Sun).

Ottoman Turks took over in 1534 (MC inconjunct Mars; ASC

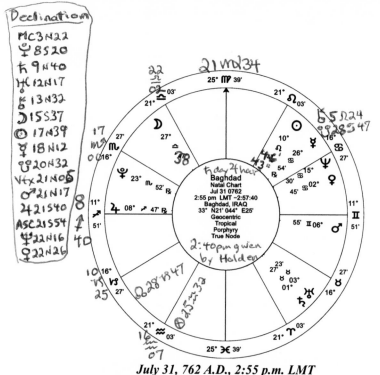

July 31, 762 A.D., 2:55 p.m. LMT
Source: Chronicles of Ancient Kingdoms by al-Biruni says early af-
ternoon of Jumada I in 145 AH. Chart rectified. Encyclopedia of Is-
lam gives August 2, 762 A.D.

opposition Neptune) and virtually ignored the city for the next four centuries. The British captured Baghdad from the Turks in 1917 (MC conjunct Pluto; ASC trine Mars). When Iraq gained independence from Britain in 1932, Baghdad remained its capital. During the first Gulf War in 1991, Baghdad was bombed by missiles (MC sextile Jupiter; ASC opposition Pluto inconjunct Moon sextile Mercury). When the U.S. invaded in March 2003, Baghdad was again the focus of fighting both between U.S. and Iraqi troops as well as repeated car bombings and sniper attacks from local insurgents (ASC opposition Jupiter).

Baghdad is a city of five million living in an area of 25 square miles on both banks of the Tigris. A metropolitan government was formed in September 1921.

56

Israel
Medinat Yisra'El

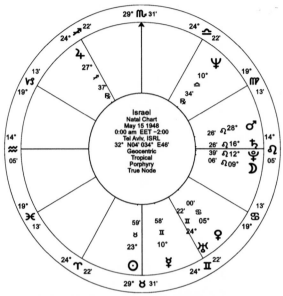

May 15, 1948, 12:00 a.m. EET, Tel Aviv.
Source: Birth time is for the end of the British Mandate. The Jerusa-
lem Post says Ben Gurion proclaimed independence at 4:00 p.m.
Other sources give the time as 4:37 p.m. when the speech was over.

Around 2000 B.C., the Hebrews under the leadership of Abraham came to this region then known as Canaan. Four centuries
later they were sold into slavery in Egypt where they remained for
another four centuries until Moses led them out of Egypt during
the Exodus. About 1000 B.C., King David united Palestine and his
son, Solomon, ruled during the Golden Age of Israel (961-922
B.C.). Assyrians destroyed the region in 722 B.C. and the Babylonians captured Judea in 587 B.C. and took its residents to Babylon.
This began the diaspora (dispersal) of the Jews from their homeland. An independent Jewish state was founded by Judas
Maccabeus in 165 B.C. but it was short-lived.

57

The Romans came in the 1st century B.C. and appointed King Herod as their king. During his reign (about 7 B.C.), Jesus Christ was born. A revolt against Roman rule erupted in 66 A.D. which destroyed the Second Temple (the first was wrecked by the Babylonians). The Jews last stand was made at Masada in 73 A.D. whereby the occupants committed suicide rather than surrender to the Roman army.

In 636 A.D., Arabs invaded this ancient land, a place sacred not only to the Jews and Christians but also to the Moslems. For the next nine centuries, the Holy Land was fought over during several religious crusades to free the region from the Moslems. In 1517, Palestine fell to the Ottoman Turks whose yoke lasted for the next four centuries. In 1920, Jordan was separated from Palestine which then became a British mandate. Britain issued the Balfour Declaration which guaranteed a homeland for the Jewish people. After the holocaust of World War II, thousands of refugees fled Europe for Palestine despite Arab warnings of impending rebellion should a Jewish state be established.

On May 14, 1948, Prime Minister David Ben Gurion proclaimed the independence of Israel. The mandate was to end that day at midnight, on a Saturday and the Sabbath, whereby no political stuff could occur. At midnight when the British mandate ended, Arab armies invaded Israel and the first conflict began which was to last a year (MC square Mars; ASC opposition Saturn/Pluto and sesquare Venus/Uranus). In October 1956, the Second Arab-Israeli war began when Israel invaded the Gaza Strip and the Sinai. Egypt had also nationalized the Suez Canal, thus denying free passage to Jews wishing to visit Israel (MC trine Moon; ASC square Sun trine Uranus).

The Third Arab-Israeli war began in June 1967 and lasted for only six days, but at its conclusion, Israel occupied the eastern half of Jerusalem, the Gaza Strip, the Sinai peninsula, the Golan Heights as well as the West Bank of the Jordan (ASC trine Mercury inconjunct Neptune). The Fourth and final Arab-Israeli war erupted in October 1973 on Yom Kippur and would precipitate a worldwide oil embargo (MC opposition Uranus).

In November 1977, Egyptian President Anwar Sadat went to Jerusalem to meet with Prime Minister Menachem Begin trying to end three decades of conflict (MC conjunct Jupiter trine Mars; ASC square Uranus). A treaty between the two nations was signed in March 1979 and soon after, Israel began withdrawing from the Sinai. Stability in the region was periodically threatened by the PLO under Yasir Arafat who had vowed to establish a new state called Palestine. Many Palestinians had fled to Jordan while others live in the West Bank or,in refugee camps in the Gaza Strip. The current crisis, called the Infitada, began in late 1988 (MC inconjunct Moon; ASC trine Pluto). Requests for Israel to vacate settlements in the West Bank have fallen on deaf ears until recently.

During the Gulf War in early 1991, Iraq fired Scud missiles at Israel (MC inconjunct Moon and Mercury square Neptune; ASC trine Saturn) hitting the city of Tel Aviv several times. Peace talks in Sept. 1993 resulted in Israel recognizing the PLO as the legal representative of the Palestinian people and the PLO recognized Israel's right to exist (MC inconjunct Pluto sesquare Mars). In July 1994, Israel signed a peace treaty with Jordan ending a 46 year-old state of war (MC inconjunct Mars/Saturn). Prime Minister Rabin was shot in November 1995 by an Orthodox Jew (ASC sextile Uranus).

Israel pulled out its troops from southern Lebanon in May 2000 and in March 2001, the hardliner, Ariel Sharon, became Prime Minister (MC inconjunct Mars/Pluto). During the latter half of 2001, terrorist bombings increased and Israel launched an offensive against the terrorists (ASC semisquare Mercury/Uranus).

In November 2004, Yasir Arafat, leader of the PLO, died in his compound in Ramallah (MC inconjunct Uranus).

Israel is a country of six million people living in an area of 8,000 square miles, about the size of Massachusetts or New Jersey. If one includes the occupied territories, Israel's size increases by 40 percent. Over 85 percent of the inhabitants are Jewish, the remainder are Arabic. Israel lies at the eastern end of the Mediterranean. From a narrow coastal strip, the land rises to the Judean plateau and then falls sharply down to the Jordan River which empties into the lowest spot on earth, the Dead Sea, which at 1,300 feet below sea level is 10 times as salty as the ocean. In the south is the Negev desert which the Israelis have partially turned into a productive agricultural region. In the north is the Sea of Galilee.

Jerusalem

Situated 30 miles from the Mediterranean and 20 miles from the Dead Sea on a high plateau, Jerusalem (city of peace) was conquered by King David around 1000 B.C. who made it his capital. His son, Solomon, built the First Temple which was destroyed by the Babylonians in 586 B.C. The Second Temple was destroyed by the Romans in 70 A.D. After the Arab conquest in 632 A.D., the Moslems built their Dome of the Rock on the site of those two former Jewish temples, a sore spot to this day. Jerusalem was captured by Crusaders at the end of the 11th century but recaptured by Saladin in 1187. Jerusalem became the capital of Israel again in 1950 after the first Israeli war.

Jerusalem is a city revered and holy to Jews, Christians and Moslems. Inside the Old City is the Wailing Wall, sacred to the Jews, the Al Aqsa Mosque, revered, by the Moslems, and the Via Dolorosa and the Church of the Holy Sepulchre, the reputed burial place of Jesus Christ. Outside the old walls is Mount Zion, the burial place of King David and the place where Christ ate his Last Supper. In Mea Shearim are tombs of the Kings of Judah. East of the Old City (which was once part of Jordan) is the Mount of Olives, sight of the Garden of Gethsemane. West of Jerusalem at En Karem is the birthplace of John the Baptist.

Tel Aviv

Tel Aviv is situated on the Mediterranean coast, a modern-looking city and the most cosmopolitan and sophisticated community in Israel. It was here in May 1948 that David Ben Gurion proclaimed the independence of Israel some eight hours before the end of the British Mandate (MC sextile Neptune; ASC trine Sun/Venus). In 1950, the ancient port of Jaffa was annexed to Tel

60

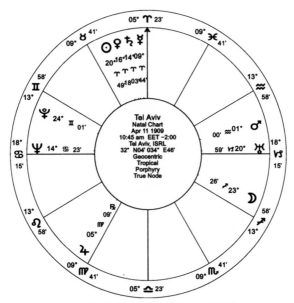

April 11, 1909, 10:45 a.m. EET
Source: General Archives; chart rectified.

Aviv and the government offices moved to Jerusalem. Due to the fact that most countries do not recognize Jerusalem as the legal capital, Tel Aviv still has most of the foreign embassies.

As the most important commercial and industrial city in Israel, during the Persian Gulf War in early 1991 it was repeatedly bombed by Iraqi Scud missiles and kept the populace in fear (progressed Sun square Mercury; MC conjunct Pluto opposition Moon; ASC square Moon and Pluto). Israel's main international airport (Lod) is located just south of the city.

Japan
Nihon

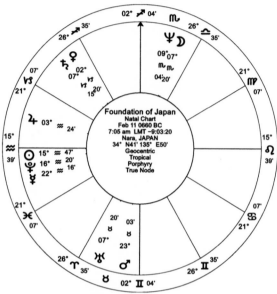

February 11, 660 B.C., Nara, 7:05 a.m. (sunrise)
Source: Research by Geoffrey Cornelius

According to legend, the foundation of the Japanese monarchy dates to February 11, 660 B.C., when Emperor Jimmu ascended the throne. With the Sun on the ASC, Japan became the "land of the rising Sun." In actuality, the foundation of the monarchy probably took place sometime in the 5th century A. D. around the time the Chinese brought their system of picture-writing to these islands and Buddhism was introduced into this land where the chief religion had been Shinto. In 1192, a feudal system was established under the Shoguns, or military dictators, which outstripped the power of the emperors. This was the age of the Samurai warriors and civil wars reigned until 1598, when the Shogun Tokugawa took over. His offspring ruled the country until the Meiji restoration in the mid-19th century.

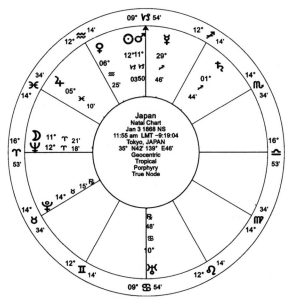

January 3, 1868, 11:55 a.m. LMT, Tokyo
Source: Tokyo University Library for the date; time rectified.

In 1274, the Mongol Emperor, Kublai Khan, tried to invade Japan but was driven away by a typhoon. The first Europeans to visit were the Portuguese who arrived in 1542. Seven years later, Francis Xavier introduced Christianity to the islands. The capital was moved from Kyoto to Tokyo in 1603, and shortly afterward Japan began to turn inward and shut out the outside world. When Perry visited Yokohama in 1853, trade negotiations began. During the previous two and a half centuries (a Pluto cycle), all foreign influence was eradicated and the Japanese were forbidden to talk or deal with any outsider. Society had become rigid and four main castes emerged at this time: the Samurai, merchants, artisans and the peasants.

On January 3, 1868, the Meiji emperor decided to take back his throne from the Shoguns who had ruled Japan for the previous seven centuries. He old ways were thrown out, feudalism was abolished and Japan decided to enter the modern age. On February 11, 1889, a constitution was presented to the emperor and a bicameral legislature was opened (Sunn and MC sextile Saturn).

Japan, feeling her oats, attacked China in 1894, and after victory the following year took the island of Formosa (Taiwan) and the Pescadores (MC conjunct Venus; ASC semi-square Uranus, Moon and Neptune). Japan attacked Port Arthur in February 1904 (ASC trine Venus), thus beginning the Russo-Japanese War. U.S. President Roosevelt negotiated a peace treaty the following year. In September 1923, the city of Tokyo was rocked by a massive earthquake and numerous fires which killed 143,000 and left one and a half million people homeless. By the time Emperor Hirohito assumed the throne in 1926, Japan had become the third-largest naval power on Earth (Sun sextile Mars trine Uranus; ASC semi-square Pluto).

Japan invented an incident against China so that it could conquer Manchuria in September 1931 to house Japan's ever-increasing population (MC sextile Pluto; ASC trine Jupiter). Japan attacked mainland China in July 1937, and began an eight-year occupation of the world's most populous nation (MC semi-square Venus). By 1939, Japan had signed a treaty with Nazi Germany and Fascist Italy, thus making Japan a member of the Axis and an enemy of the Allied forces during World War II (ASC conjunct Uranus).

Japan had designed a plan to conquer all of southeast Asia, but in order to succeed, it had to attack all points simultaneously. Thus on December 7, 1941, Japan attacked the naval base at Pearl Harbor on the island of Oahu in the Hawaiian Islands; the following day the U.S. declared war on Japan (ASC square Moon and Neptune opposition Sun and Mars). By the end of 1944, horrendous casualties piled up but the Japanese refused to surrender.

American warplanes began to bomb Tokyo in early 1945, laying waste to the city that only 22 years before had been devastated by an earthquake. In August 1945, the first atomic bomb was dropped on Hiroshima; three days later another bomb was dropped, this time on Nagasaki. The Japanese gave up August 15, 1945, and Douglas MacArthur accepted the Japanese capitulation September 1, 1945 on the deck of the USS Missouri in Tokyo Bay

(Suns square Mercury; MC semi-square Pluto; ASC sextile Pluto). More than one and a half million Japanese had died in the war, and now it was time to rebuild the nation.

MacArthur became the de-facto ruler of Japan after the war. Numerous reforms were made, including giving women the vote. The new constitution of May 1947 was based on American principles; the Emperor lost his divinity and became a figurehead; a parliamentary system of government began; and the military was restricted (Sun trine Saturn; MC sesquare Mercury; ASC sesquare Saturn). America finally pulled out April 28, 1952, and Japanese sovereignty was restored (Sun sextile Venus; ASC sesquare Jupiter). Okinawa was returned to Japan in May 1972, but the U.S. retained the right to house military bases on the island.

In the summer of 1990, the Japanese began to enter a recession from which it has yet to recover (Sun conjunct Pluto sesquare Mercury). The Nikkei index fell from 40,000 to 10,000, a loss of 75 percent. Japanese real estate prices began to plummet and business interests in other countries were sold. The Japanese economic resurgence after the war had been spectacular as it was now the largest industrial nation in Asia and the third-largest economic power on Earth. Goods produced in Japan were cheaper than those made in America and often of better quality. Where would we be today had not the Japanese made transistor radios, high-quality televisions and more fuel-efficient automobiles? Despite the economic downturn in the 1990s, the unemployment rate was a measly two and a half percent, something the Japanese considered way too high. Japanese workers stay longer with their companies than do Americans, possibly due to excellent relations between business and labor. Another factor might be the homogenity of Japan: 99 percent of Japan is Japanese and natives are taught to think and act for the good of the country.

In January 1995, a massive earthquake shook the city of Kobe, killing 5,000 people and causing $90 billion in damage. Two months later, a sarin gas attack in the Tokyo subway was blamed on a religious cult; 12 people were killed and thousands injured.

Japan consists of four main islands: Honshu, Hokkaido,

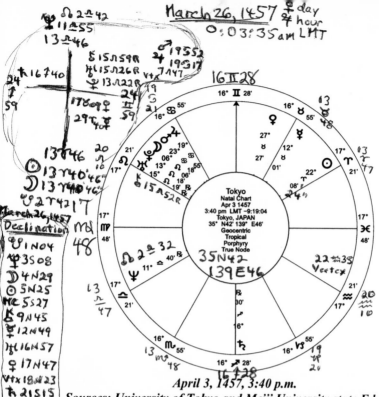

March 26, 1457 ☿ day ☿ hour
0:03:35am LMT

Tokyo
Natal Chart
Apr 3 1457
3:40 pm LMT −9:19:04
Tokyo, JAPAN
35° N42' 139° E46'
Geocentric
Tropical
Porphyry
True Node

April 3, 1457, 3:40 p.m.

Sources: University of Tokyo and Meiji University state Edo was founded in April 1457. Date and time speculative and rectified.

Shikoku and Kyushu. About 125 million people live in an area the size of California. Over 70 percent of the country is mountainous and only five percent of the land is arable. Practically everything has to be imported because Japan has few natural resources. This makes Tokyo one of the world's most-expensive cities, and its metropolitan area of nearly 25 million the largest in the world.

Tokyo

First settled in the mid 12th century near what is now the district of Asakusa, the village was known as Edo after its founder. With the arrival of Ota Dokan in 1457, a castle was built to fortify his domain. Edo remained a sleepy fishing village until the arrival of the Shogun in 1603 (MC square Moon) and almost overnight, Edo was transformed into a metropolis of 100,000, 75 percent of them being Samurai and their families. To insure the dominance of Edo over Kyoto, the capital of Japan, the Shogun required the Daimyo

66

♂ 15♏51 STATION ret April 6 9:04:04am LMT
♅ 15♏16 STATION ret April 14 2:21:04am LMT
☿ 18♌18 STATION ret April 15 7:14:04am LMT
♀ 13♏16 STATION ret April 16 12:36:04pm LMT

(counselors) to live part of the year in Edo, a tradition which lasted until the Meiji Restoration in 1868. Tokyo had been the world's largest city since 1720 when it reached a population of one million people.

Through the centuries earthquakes and fires have periodically leveled the city with the result that Tokyo has been rebuilt on the average of every 11 years since its founding. The quakes of 1633 (MC sesquare Mars), 1650 (MC conjunct Mars) 1703 (ASC sextile Moon) and 1855 (ASC square Mars) were quite severe. Due to the profusion of wooden structures, fires were also a constant threat. The conflagrations of 1657 (MC and ASC sesquare Uranus/Pluto) and 1682 (ASC inconjunct Neptune) killed more than 100,000 each time. In 1707, Mt. Fuji erupted, sending tons of debris across the countryside and burying Tokyo in six inches of soot (ASC trine Neptune).

With the Meiji Restoration of 1868 (MC conjunct Moon), the shogunate was ousted and the emperor moved the capital from Kyoto to Edo, which was renamed Tokyo. Four years later the Ginza was ravaged by fire and the first railroad to the port city of Yokohama completed (MC sextile Neptune square Mercury). The vast railway system of Japan received its impetus in 1910, when the Yamanote line which encircles central Tokyo was completed (ASC sesquare Jupiter). The worst calamity ever to befall this city occurred on September 1, 1923, when an earthquake hit the surrounding Kanto plain (ASC conjunct Saturn, MC semi-square Uranus/Pluto). The following firestorms devastated 25 square miles, killed 143,000 people, burned more than 700,000 houses and left one and a half million people homeless, or about 60 percent of the total population. Most of the damage wasn't caused by the quake but from the 450 fires which were spawned by the numerous wood stoves then in operation for the noon meal. But Tokyo was completely rebuilt in seven years, just in time for the emergence of the worldwide depression.

During the early years of World War II, General Doolittle oversaw the bombing of the city (MC square Jupiter), but that was nothing compared with the intense aerial bombardment of March

1945. More than 250,000 were killed, 800,000 buildings destroyed, two million made homeless and requiring four and a half million to flee (ASC sesquare Uranus/Pluto). Little remained in the central part of Tokyo and for miles around, there was only desolation and total destruction. During the American occupation, Tokyo was again rebuilt and was well on her way to regaining the title of premier city of the Orient. The first of many expressways was begun in 1962 and the height limit of 102ft. was repealed. The bullet train was inaugurated in 1964, just in time for the Olympics (ASC opposition Jupiter).

Tokyo is a city of contrasts, infinite variety and boundless vitality. Often reckless and raw-boned, it pulsates with excitement and drive unmatched by any other city in the world. You either love or hate Tokyo, but you can't ignore it. Tokyo is unique in that it looks like most other western metropolises, but in order to savour the Oriental flavour, one must look into the alleys in its many neighborhoods to find its true nature. One would quickly find that there are more than 190 colleges here along with five symphony orchestras and three opera companies. More than 500 cinemas dot the city with an equal number of night clubs and cabarets. Tokyo has more than 50,000 restaurants, more per capita than any large city on Earth. It also has the world's largest police force which might explain the lowest per capita crime rate on the planet. One can feel safe and secure anywhere, anytime; it might also be because the Japanese have been forced to get along with each other due to their crowded living conditions. Who knows?

Like Houston in America, Tokyo has no zoning laws, so elegant structures abut dismal shacks that could be called harmony in the extreme. Natives live in cramped quarters, about half a square meter per person, four percent of the space allotted to those living in Manhattan, America's most crowded community. Tokyo is in desperate need of more open space: its parks are crowded to the hilt as it has only one-tenth the green spaces as does London. One can't complain that the streets take up much space as only 11 percent of the city is paved over compared with 35 percent in New York. Tokyo thus relies heavily on mass transport and has the busiest rail

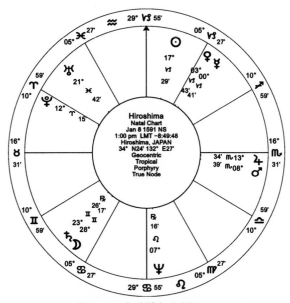

January 8, 1591, 1:00 p.m.
Source: Prefecture Library; time rectified.

station in the world through which one and a half million commuters pass each day. About 2,500 trains depart and arrive each day, five times more than in New York. Traffic moves at a snail's pace and it's often faster to walk than ride in a car or taxi.

Hiroshima

Situated in western Honshu on the Ota river delta at the western end of the Inland Sea. This city is famous for being the site of the world's first atomic bomb detonation over a populated area on August 6, 1945. More than 200,000 people were killed and 80 percent of the city was reduced to ashes in the firestorm that followed.

Kyoto

Situated 30 miles northeast of Osaka near the southern end of Lake Biwako in central Honshu, it was the Imperial Capital of Japan for more than 1,000 years until the government moved to Tokyo in 1868. Kyoto is Japan's treasure-house of art and culture as

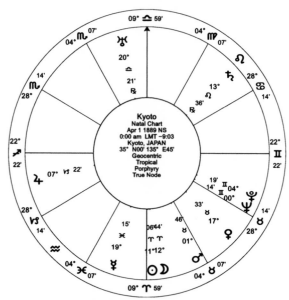

April 1, 1889, 12:00 a.m.
Source: Kyoto Library.

the temples, shrines and museums will attest. Fortunately, it escaped damage during World War II.

Nagasaki April 9, 1571 05 Nam

This city was the only point of contact between Japan and the outside world, a place where Christianity was allowed during its first century. After 1637, all foreigners with the exception of Dutch traders, were banned from Japan and persecution of Christians began. Chinese merchants were allowed to trade on a small island in the bay. Nagasaki was reopened to the West only in 1859. Situated in the western end of the island of Kyushu, its shipbuilding and manufacturing industries made it the target of the second atomic bomb attack on August 9, 1945. More than 50,000 people were killed but only 40 percent of the city was decimated.

Mayor Killed April 17, 2007

Nagoya

Situated on Honshu island 175 miles southwest of Tokyo,

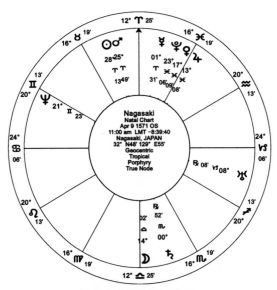

April 9, 1571, 11:00 a.m.
Source: Prefecture Library; time rectified.

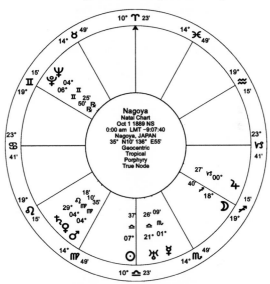

October 1, 1889, 12:00 a.m.
Source: University Library.

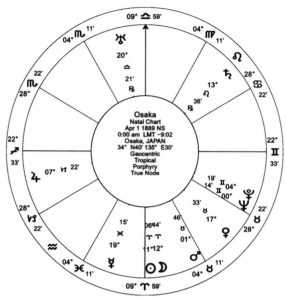

April 1, 1889, 12:00 a.m.
Source: Kansai University.

Nagoya was heavily bombed during World War II due to its numerous manufacturing establishments.

Osaka

Osaka is Japan's third largest city after Tokyo and Yokohama and sits at the delta of the Yodo river at the eastern end of the Inland Sea, 250 miles southwest of Tokyo. It's an industrial city with the world's first offshore airport. More than 1,000 bridges span the river, making it the Venice of Japan. Parts of the city are in danger of sinking due to land subsidence. The most famous sight in Osaka is the Castle originally built in the 17th century and restored in 1931. Osaka is also famous for its nightlife and hedonistic ways.

Jordan
Al-Mamlakal Al-Urdunniyah
Al-Hashimiyah

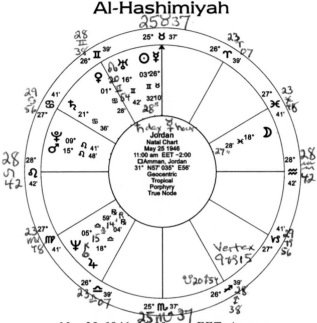

May 25, 1946, 11:00 a.m. EET, Amman
Source: Isaac Starkman says 11:00 a.m. New York Times says
"morning."

Jordan occupies the land east of the Jordan River which empties into the Dead Sea, the lowest place on earth at 1312 feet below sea level. The Dead Sea is 10 times as salty as the ocean and one can float in it with no need of a life jacket. Jordan is mostly desert and has a very short coastline on the Red Sea at Aqaba. Its five million people (half of them Palestinian) live in an area the size of Indiana or Portugal.

This region in ancient times was conquered by Egyptians, Assyrians, Chaldeans, Persians and Romans. Arabs invaded in 636 A.D. and the Ottoman Turks took over in 1517. The British gained the mandate over Trans-Jordan in 1920 and a monarchy

73

was formed the following year. After World War II, the British pulled out and Jordan was independent.

Jordan fought against newly-formed Israel in May 1948 and annexed East Jerusalem and the West Bank of the Jordan (progressed ASC sextile Venus). In June 1967, it lost those previous gains to Israel during the Six-Day War (progressed MC sextile Mars; progressed ASC square Uranus). In 1988, Jordan gave up all claims to East Jerusalem and the West Bank (progressed ASC conjunct Neptune) and signed a peace treaty with Israel in October 1994 (progressed ASC sextile Pluto). King Hussein died in February 1999.

Amman

Situated 25 miles northeast of the Dead Sea, it was first settled about 4000 B.C. It was renamed Philadelphia during Roman times and was conquered by Arabs in 635 A.D. By 1300, Amman had disappeared altogether. Resettled in 1878 by Russians and made capital of TransJordan in 1921.

Kazakstan
Qazaqstan Respublikasy

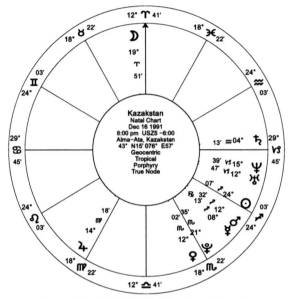

December 16, 1991, 8:00 p.m., Alma Ata
Source: Astrologer Jacob Schwartz.

During the 13th century, the Mongols ruled this vast region. Various Khans ruled from the 15th century an empire of nomads until the Russians took over in 1731 and abolished the khanates. Kazakstan became part of the Soviet Union in 1936. Independence came in 1991. and four years later, private ownership of land was approved. The capital was moved from Alma Ata (Almaty) to Astana out inthe middle of nowhere in June 1998 (progressed ASC opposition Saturn).

Kazakstan is a huge country, more than one million square miles in area (four times the size of Texas or Ukraine). It has only 15 million people, however, and only 40 percent are Kazaks; an equal number are Russian. This huge nation borders the Caspian Sea (elevation 433 feet below sea level), the dividing line between

75

Europe and Asia. Inside the country is Lake Balkhash and the Aral Sea which has shrunk to half of its former size due to massive irrigation projects. Kazakstan was also the site of the Soviet Union's space launch program and has numerous nuclear weapons depots in the region.

Alma Ata (Almaty)

Founded as a military post in 1854 by the Russians, it grew rapidly after completion of the Turkestan-Siberian railway. It was rebuilt after the devastating earthquakes of 1887 and 1911.

North Korea
Choson Minjujuui In-min Konghwaguk

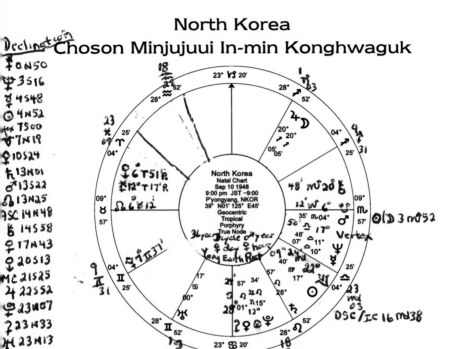

September 10, 1948, 9:00 p.m. KST, Pyongyang
Source: Radio broadcast (see American Astrology, August 1994).

Prior to the establishment of the People's Republic in September 1948, this nation's history is identical to that of its southern neighbor. A Soviet-backed Communist government attained power in May 1948 and assumed full power four months later under Kim il-Sung. Two years later in June 1950, North Korean troops invaded South Korea across the Yalu river at the 38th parallel and the Korean War began (ASC inconjunct Neptune). When the armistice was finally signed in June 1953, the 38th parallel was made the boundary between these two nations (MC inconjunct Saturn; ASC trine Sun square Pluto semisquare Uranus).

In 1968, the North Koreans captured the USS Pueblo which it accused of spying; its crew was imprisoned for one year (ASC inconjunct Mars). Four years later, Kim il-Sung was declared pres-

77

ident for life (MC inconjunct Sun; ASC trine Mercury). When South Korea established relations with China in August 1992, North Korea became alarmed and began to go into hibernation, feeling cut off from the world (ASC semisquare Pluto). In March 1993, North Korea withdrew from the nuclear proliferation treaty (ASC conjunct Uranus). After ruling this country for 46 years, Kim il-Sung died in July 1994 and was succeeded by his son, Kim Jong-il. A conference between North and South Korea in June 2000 ended some U.S. sanctions. This country has been in the midst of a severe famine for many years now and more than three million are reputed to have died. Whether this is due to meteorological anomalies or just mismanagement of the economy by the government has yet to be confirmed.

North Korea has a very difficult chart. First, there's Mars squaring Venus, rulers of the ASC and DSC are inharmonious, not a good sign for equable relationships with other countries. Then there's the Sun square Moon and Jupiter, the midpoint of which is Mars. Mercury conjunct Neptune doesn't know what's going on, or maybe doesn't even care. This is a hilly and mountainous country where 20 million live in an area the size of New York. The capital is Pyongyang, which was founded in 1122 B.C. as Heijo on the site of the former capital of the Tangun dynasty.

Pyongyang

Reputed to be the oldest city in Korea, it's situated on the Taedon River 55 miles from the ocean. The Chinese founded the city named Lolang in 108 B.C. It was heavily bombed during the Korean War. The new city built since then has broad boulevards with numerous parks and open spaces, but little motor traffic.

South Korea
Taehan Minguk

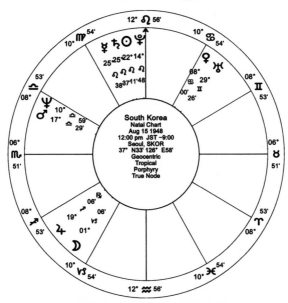

August 15, 1948, noon KST, Seoul
Source: New York Times, no time mentioned. Ceremony was
scheduled to begin at 11:00 a.m., but MacArthur was a bit late.

About 2300 B.C., the Tangun civilization was founded, but recorded Korean history began 15 centuries later with the establishment of a Chinese colony near Pyongyang in the north. In 668 A.D., the Silla kingdom united the region to be followed by the Koryo kingdom which ruled until 1392. They gave their name to this ancient land. The Manchus invaded in 1637 and then isolated it from the rest of the world for the next two and a half centuries.

Known as the "Hermit Kingdom" until 1867, when Japan forced Korea to open its ports to foreign trade. In 1910, Japan took over the entire country and renamed it Chosen. After World War II, Soviet troops entered the northern half while the Americans occupied the south. At the Potsdam conference in 1945, the 38th parallel was chosen to be the dividing line between the two countries. Dr. Syngman Rhee was chosen to be the first leader and he was inaugurated in August 1948.

In June 1950, North Korean troops invaded the south by crossing the Yalu River (MC conjunct Pluto sesquare Moon; ASC trine Venus). The war lasted three years until an armistice was signed (MC sextile Mars). Dr. Rhee ruled as dictator until 1960 when he was deposed (ASC square Pluto sesquare Uranus). Park Chung Hee then took over and curbed individual freedoms (MC conjunct Saturn and Mercury semi-square Neptune). Park was assassinated in October 1979 some seven years after instituting martial law (ASC inconjunct Uranus). During the years of martial law, schools were closed to prevent demonstrations, censorship was in force and a strict curfew curtailed nightlife in the capital. Student demonstrations in June 1987 against the government brought renewed tension to South Korea (MC square Jupiter). Seoul hosted the 1988 Summer Olympics. Three political parties merged in 1990 (ASC inconjunct Venus).

General Chun, who had ruled since 1979, was convicted of treason and corruption in August 1996 and sent to prison for life (MC square Uranus semisquare Pluto). Beginning in 1997, South Korea's currency and stock took a nose dive and the IMF had to bail out the country (ASC sextile Pluto). General Chun was pardoned as well soon after.

The Sun, Saturn and Pluto in the tenth house point to the very strong, willful and dictatorial men who have led this country since independence. The Sun/Saturn/Mercury conjunction also semisquares Neptune in the twelfth, pointing to the many coups and assassinations. Moon opposition Uranus might indicate the IMF bailout as both are in financial houses and Jupiter sextile Mars points to the industrial resurgence since the Korean War which has made this country economically important and resourceful.

South Korea is a land of 45 million people in an area the size of Hungary. It occupies 40 percent of the Korean peninsula, a region of rugged mountains with few natural harbors (Pusan and Inchon are the largest). Seoul became the capital in 1392.

Seoul

Situated on the Han River 35 miles from the Yellow Sea, Seoul became the capital of Korea in 1392. During the Japanese occupation (1910-1945), it was called Hansong. During the Korean War, it was invaded by Communist armies and heavily bombed. Its population shrank from more than one million to a mere 23,000. Reconstructed after the war, Seoul is now the industrial and commercial heart of the country.

Kuwait
Dawlat Al-Kuwayt

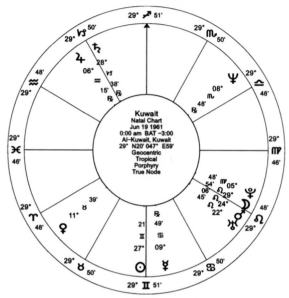

June 19, 1961, 12:00 a.m., Kuwait City
Source: New York Times, midnight assumed.

Kuwait was founded about 1740 by nomads from neighboring Arabia. In 1757, the Al-Sabah dynasty was founded which rules to this day. During the early 19th century, Britain came to the aid of this country when a strict Moslem sect, the Wahhabis, threatened to overrun the region in a holy war. Britain stayed and Kuwait came under direct British rule in 1897. Independence came in 1961.

Oil was discovered in 1938 and petroleum exporting began eight years later. Iraq invaded Kuwait in March 1973, claiming it as their own territory (MC trine Venus) but with Saudi Arabian aid, Iraq backed down. In 1982, Kuwait became the first Arab state to give women the vote (MC sesquare Pluto). Then the country became a capitalist welfare state where its people pay no taxes and the government provides free medical services, education and telephones. The generous government also subsidizes new housing and businesses; in Kuwait, one out of every 200 is a millionaire.

Kuwait was invaded by Iraq in August 1990 (MC inconjunct Sun conjunct Saturn; ASC conjunct Venus). After six weeks of war, the country was liberated by a coalition led by the U.S. The Iraqis destroyed much of the country and set fire to hundreds of oil wells. The smoke and pollution wafted all the way to India. Women were given the vote in May 2005 (MC square Venus).

Kuwait is an artificially-created country at the northwest end of the Persian Gulf. Its flat, desert-like, arid and extremely hot. The population of two and a half million lives in an area the size of Denmark. Oil is its major export and Kuwait has 25 percent of the world's proven petroleum reserves.

Kyrgyzstan
Kyrgyz Respublikasy

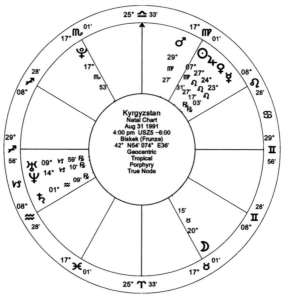

August 31, 1991, 4:00 p.m. (10:00 a.m. GMT), Bishkek
Source: Nathaly Korn of the Astro. Assn.

Kirghizia was invaded by the Mongols in 1207 and by the mid-18th century, the region had become part of the Qing Empire from China. Russia annexed the region in 1876 and it became part of the Soviet Union in 1936. Independence came in 1991. Private ownership of land was approved in October 1998 (progressed MC square Saturn; progressed ASC trine Sun sesquare Moon). Beginning in 1999, Muslim extremists began a revolt to establish an Islamic state.

This country is extremely mountainous and peaks in the Tien Shan range tower more than 24,000 feet in elevation. Only five million people live there (22 percent are Russian) in an area the size of Utah or Germany.

Laos
Sathalanalat Paxathipatai Paxaxon Lao

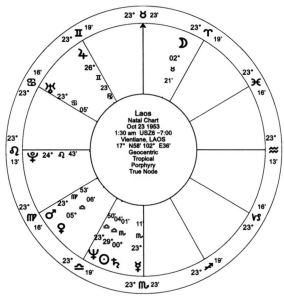

October 23, 1953, 1:30 a.m. ST, Vientiane
Source: Book of World Horoscopes by Nick Campion says treaty was
signed at 7:30 p.m., October 22, 1953 in Paris. Chart relocated

During the 12th century, this region was settled by refugee Thai tribesmen. Two centuries later, the Lan Xang kingdom was founded. By 1707, the area was split into Luang Prabang in the north and Vientians in the south. France made Laos a protectorate in 1893, but couldn't aid the Laotians when the Japanese invaded in 1941. Independence was prematurely declared in 1945, but French troops remained for another four years. Laos was then made part of the French Union.

Pathet Lao forces began fighting the Vietnamese in 1953, and France decided to pull out (MC opposition Mercury sextile Uranus square Pluto trine Mars inconjunct Neptune). In 1957, Prince Souvanna Phouma formed a coalition government, but by 1960, civil war had begun (MC inconjunct Sun and Saturn). The Pathet Lao finally withdrew in 1964 (MC trine Venus), but peace didn't really arrive until 1973, when another cease-fire was signed.

The Pathet Lao quickly proceeded to reestablish themselves and on December 3, 1975, a Republic was proclaimed and the 622-year-old monarchy was abolished (MC sesquare Sun and Saturn; ASC semi-square Sun). Over the next few years, more than 200,000 refugees fled to Thailand to escape the repressive Communist regime.

Laos is a country of five million people living in an area the size of England and Scotland combined. Over 80 percent of the country is jungle, the climate is hot and humid. The Mekong River flows through the western part of the country. The capital is Vientiane.

Vientiane

Situated on the Mekong River opposite Thailand, during French colonial times it had the flavor of a small town in France. Even though it's the capital of a Communist nation, its 30 pagodas have been retained.

Lebanon
Al-Jumhuriyah Al-Lubnaniyah

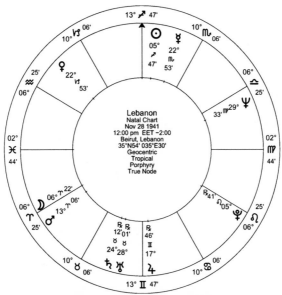

Lebanon
Natal Chart
Nov 28 1941
12:00 pm EET −2:00
Beirut, Lebanon
35°N54' 035°E30'
Geocentric
Tropical
Porphyry
True Node

November 26, 1941, noon EET, Beirut
Sources: The Times of London implies midnight. Nicholas Campion
says proclamation took place during the day. Noon presumed.

Known in ancient times as Phoenicia, this region sent sailors
throughout the known world and established colonies in North Africa and as far away as Great Britain. The civilization reached its
peak around 1000 B.C. and its capital, Tyre, was the largest city in
the eastern Mediterranean. Over the centuries, Phoenicia was cov-
eted by Persians, Assyrians, Babylonians, Egyptians and Greeks
from Macedonia.

During the 1st century B.C., Phoenicia became a Roman province and was administered from neighboring Syria. After the fall
of the Roman Empire in the 5th century A.D., the region sank into
oblivion for the next thousand years until the Ottoman Turks captured in 1516 and then virtually ignored the area for the next four

87

centuries. Lebanon became independent from Turkey in 1920, but then came under French mandate until November 1941, when the French gave up the territory. Note the independence chart has Mars trine the Midheaven but the Moon squares it as well. Having the last degree of Aquarius on the Ascendant doesn't help one bit, in my opinion.

Two years later, in November 1943, the Lebanese were angry that the French weren't letting them run their own country (ASC square Sun). The French finally left and pulled out their troops in 1946 (ASc semi-square Venus inconjunct Pluto). U.S. Marines were sent in in May 1958, when a Syrian-aided revolt erupted (MC inconjunct Uranus square Neptune). Israel began to attack guerrilla camps in Lebanon in 1970 (MC sesquare Saturn; ASC sextile Jupiter). Five years later, in April 1975, a civil war broke out (MC = Venus/Mars; ASC semisquare Moon). Over the next two years, more than 60,000 were killed and damage ran into the billions. Beirut was severely damaged during this conflict between Christians and Moslems. Syria intervened in 1976 and fought the PLO. By 1981, Syria was fighting the Christians and then two Moslem sects began fighting as well. Israel began air raids (ASC square Pluto).

In June 1982, Israel invaded PLO camps but withdrew the following year (MC trine Saturn). Syria remained, however, to watch over the region. A treaty with Syria was signed in May 1991 even though Syria still stuck its nose into Lebanon's affairs (Mc sextile Sun sesquare Jupiter).

Israel bombed southern Lebanon in 1993 (MC opposition Pluto; ASC conjunct Saturn). Israel finally removed its troops from Lebanon in May 2000 (MC sextile Mars). In February 2005, Prime Minister Hariri was assassinated and neighboring Syria was blamed (MC sesquare Neptune). Syria wisely withdrew most of its troops shortly afterward. In December 2005, a Lebanese publisher and politician critical of the Syrian regime was gunned down in Beirut.

Lebanon is a land of four million people living in an area the size of Connecticut or one-third the size of Belgium. A narrow

88

coastal strip along the Mediterranean rises up sharply and two mountain ranges flank the Bekaa valley. Ethnically, 90 percent of the people are Arabs but only 60 percent are Moslem. There's a sizeable Christian minority (35 percent) and a small but very vocal Druze minority.

Beirut

Founded by the Phoenicians in the 14th century B.C., it was an important Greek and Roman trading center. During the Crusades, it fell to Saladin in the late 12th century and to the Ottoman Turks four centuries later. Beirut became the capital of Lebanon in 1920 under the French mandate. Beirut was called the "Paris of the East" and prospered as the chief financial and trade center of the Middle East. It was also a major center of learning due to its four universities. All that changed in 1975 when the civil war began which took a heavy toll on the city. Business came to a halt and the city was split in two by the Green Line. Moslems lived in the west, Christians in the east. Economic recovery didn't arrive until the mid 1990s.

Malaysia

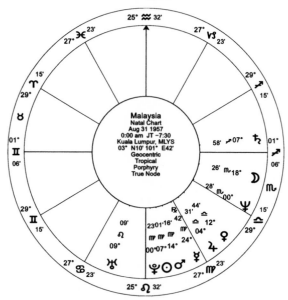

Malaysia
Natal Chart
Aug 31 1957
0:00 am JT -7:30
Kuala Lumpur, MLYS
03° N10' 101° E42'
Geocentric
Tropical
Porphyry
True Node

August 31, 1957, 12:00 a.m., Kuala Lumpur
Source: Perpustakaan Negara Malaysia states that
independence came at midnight.

Prior to the arrival of the Portuguese in 1511, not much was known about this country. In 1592, the British East India Co. came to Penang and formally took control of Sumatra in 1786. By the 20th century, Britain held sway over the entire Malay peninsula but there was strong resistance to British domination. For this reason, Britain made Sabah, Sarawak and Brunei protectorates in 1888. During World War II, the Japanese occupied all of Malaya. After the war, the Union of Malaya was formed.

Malaya was granted independence by Britain in August 1957. Malaysia was formed in 1963 and contained the city-state of Singapore (MC inconjunct Jupiter; ASC opposition Saturn). Due to differing political aspirations, Singapore seceded from Malaysia two years later (MC opposition Sun; ASC sextile Uranus). In 1969, riots between the native Malays and the majority Chinese who were considered foreigners precipitated 21 months of martial law (ASC square Mars).

Like many divided countries, Malaysia has Gemini rising. Despite the Sun-Saturn square, political life doesn't seem to have the intensity or provoke radical elements that one might suspect in other Asian nations. Uranus rules the MC and it makes several benefic aspects indicating a usually harmonious transfer of power from one government to another with little threat of military coups.

Malaysia is a land of 23 million people about half the size of France. The peninsula is divided by high mountains and has dense jungles. Malaysia also contains the regions of Sabah and Sarawak on the island of Borneo. The capital is Kuala Lumpur which was founded in 1857.

Kuala Lumpur

Sitting at the confluence of the Kelang and Gombak rivers 20

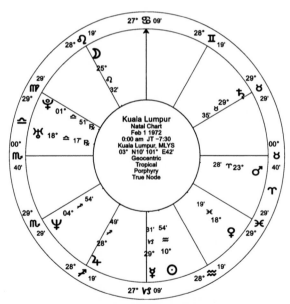

February 1, 1972, 12:00 a..m.
Source: Perpustakaan Negara Malaysia

miles from the Straits of Malacca, it was founded in 1857 as a tin-mining camp. It was chosen to be the capital of the Malay Federated States in 1895. K.L., as it is called locally, is home to two of the world's tallest buildings, the Petronas Towers which were designed to look like two tall minarets.

Maldives
Diveli Jumhuriya

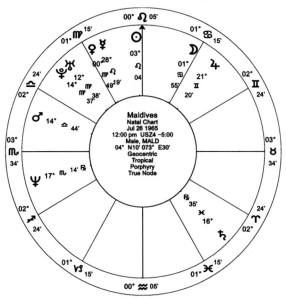

Maldives
Natal Chart
Jul 26 1965
12:00 pm USZ4 –5:00
Male, MALD
04° N10' 073° E30'
Geocentric
Tropical
Porphyry
True Node

July 26, 1965, noon, Male
Source: Book of World Horoscopes by Nicholas Campion;
Los Angeles Times says 12:0l a.m.

From the 12th century until 1965, these islands were ruled as a Sultanate. In 1153, Moslems arrived and the Portuguese came three centuries later. During the 17th century, the Maldives became a Protectorate of Ceylon. Independence came in 1965 and a Republic was formed three years later.

The Maldives consist of 19 atolls and 1,087 islands lying in the Indian Ocean. Only 215 islands are inhabited, the largest being only five square miles in area. Due to global warming and rising sea levels, the ocean could eventually completely submerge this country sometime in the near future if something radical isn't done in the next few years.

Mongolia
Mongol Uls

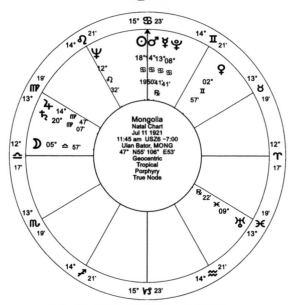

July 11, 1921, 11:45 a.m., Ulan Bator
Source: Mongolian Mission to the United Nations says
"about noon." Chart rectified.

From the sands of this barren land came Genghis Khan who was elected in 1206 to lead his people to glory and empire. The Mongol Empire would eventually range from the Danube to China and from Siberia to the Persian Gulf. During the 15th century, the Chinese repelled the Mongols and by the 1590s, Inner Mongolia had become occupied by the Chinese. The northern part was annexed by the Manchu dynasty in 1691.

When the revolution in China erupted in October 1911, Mongolia declared its independence from the Manchus but China didn't recognize it. A treaty was signed the following year with Russia but the Russians didn't recognize Mongolia's independence either. A pro-Soviet coup took place in March 1921 and four months later, Mongolia gained its freedom.

The first leader was Sukhe Bator but he was assassinated two years later by Choibalsan who proclaimed a People's Republic in 1924 (MC conjunct Sun; ASC trine Mars). Choibalsan would rule as a Stalinist type of dictator until his death in 1952. Mongolia collectivized all livestock, ending private ownership of their most-prized possessions (MC semisquare Moon; ASC trine Uranus and Pluto). The government had already closed most of Mongolia's monasteries in the 1930s and many lamas were shot. In 1962, a railroad was completed that linked Mongolia to both Moscow and Peking (ASC trine Mercury square Neptune). During 1983, it was reported that the government was ousting non-native Chinese (MC conjunct Jupiter/Saturn ASC sesquare Mars).

Mongolia is a land of about two million people living in an area three times the size of France. The region is sparsely populated and most live near the capital city. The Gobi desert occupies the southern half of the country while high steppes are found in the west. The center consists of a high plateau on which nomads live as they have for centuries tending their flocks and living in circular tents called yurts.

Nepal
Nepal Adhirajya

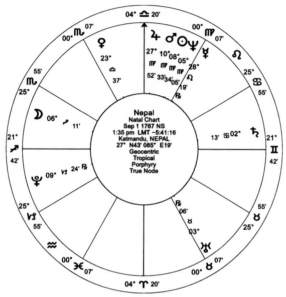

September 1, 1767, 1:35 p.m., Katmandu
*Source: Embassy of Nepal says the dynasty took over during a reli-
gious festival. Chart rectified.*

Originally a land of petty principalities, Nepal was unified in
September 1767 by the Gurkhas. Nepal fought a war with neighboring Tibet in 1791 (MC semi-square Mars; ASC conjunct Pluto)
and with British India in 1814 (MC sesquare Saturn). The ruler of
the country was reduced to a mere figurehead in 1847 (MC
sesquare Uranus) by the Rana dynasty which itself was overthrown in 1951 (MC inconjunct Neptune).

A Constitutional Monarchy was proclaimed in 1959 (ASC
sesquare Sun) and four years later, polygamy, child marriage and
the caste systems were abolished (ASC sextile Jupiter). In 1990, a
new Constitution restricted royal authority and a Parliament was
formed (MC semi-square Saturn; ASC sextile Venus). Tragedy

96

came to the royal family in June 2001, when the King, Queen and seven other members of the royal family were shot by the Crown Prince who later shot himself because his father kept interfering in his choice of a bride (MC square Mercury). Five months later, a state of emergency was declared due to rebellion among the Maoists.

Nepal is a picturesque land located on the southern foothills of the Himalayas. Many mountains ranges make communication and travel quite difficult between one region and another but the south has fertile valleys and is the source of the mighty Ganges River. More than 25 million people live in this region the size of England or Illinois. The capital is Katmandu, which was founded in 723 A.D.

The highly-religious and spiritual nature of the Nepalese can be shown by five planets in the ninth house as well as the Sun conjunct Neptune square the Moon. For years, Nepal was an isolated land not frequented by tourists due to Pluto rising and opposition seventh house Saturn. Tourism is at present one of the main sources of income, especially for climbers and hikers who desire to scale the world's highest peaks, including Mt. Everest.

Katmandu

Situated in central Nepal about 55 miles from India, it was founded in 723 A.D. and became capital after Nepal was born in 1767. During the 1960s, Katmandu became popular with hippies due to cheap drugs and a leisurely lifestyle. In the old part of the city lies the Royal Palace with more than 1,700 rooms.

Oman
Saltanat Uman

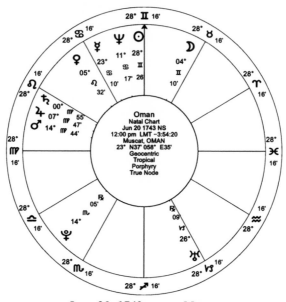

June 20, 1743, noon, Muscat
Source: Embassy of Oman cites a book in Arabic which gives the
date of 27 Rabi II, AH 1156; no time mentioned, noon presumed.

This region was an important fishing and trading area with an elaborate irrigation system 2,000 years before Christ was born. Moslem traders brought their religion to Oman in the 7th century. Vasco da Gama stopped here on his way to India in 1498 and 10 years later, Portugal conquered the region. The Portuguese were ousted by the Arabs in 1650 and by 1698, Oman had annexed Mombasa and Zanzibar. The Turks were expelled in 1741, two years before the present dynasty took control.

British friendship was formed after a treaty was signed in 1798 (MC opposition Uranus). The Omani Empire was divided in 1861, with only the island of Zanzibar continuing to pay tribute (MC square Sun trine Uranus). Oil was discovered in 1964 (MC opposi-

98

tion Neptune) and petroleum exporting began three years later.

In July 1970, the Sultan was overthrown and the country's name was changed from Muscat and Oman to simply Oman (ASC square Mercury). By 1976, 12 years of civil war ended when rebels surrendered their demands for an independent Dhofar nation (MC opposition Mercury).

Oman is a land of two and a half million people living in an area the size of Romania or Wyoming. A narrow coastal strip yields to barren mountains and a stony plateau. Oman's location at the entrance to the Persian Gulf and the Straits of Hormuz makes the stability of this nation very important to the western world. Petroleum is Oman's chief export, like most other countries in the region.

Pakistan
Islami Jamhuriyae Pakistan

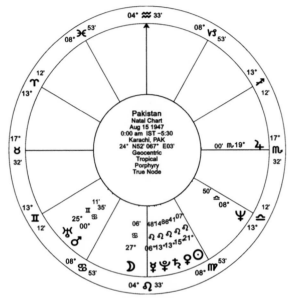

August 15, 1947, 12:00 a.m., Karachi
Source: Pakistani archives and The New York Times
both state midnight.

About 4000 B.C., one of the world's oldest civilizations sprang up on the banks off the Indus river. The Aryans invaded in 1500 B.C. and a thousand years later, Alexander the Great invaded Baluchistan on his way to India. The year was 326 B.C. and the Macedonian conqueror would go further east. The Arab invasion of 712 A.D. brought Islam to the region which would one day become part of the vast Moghul Empire during the 16th century. The British ruled this region from November 1858 and ousted the Moghuls.

In 1940, Mohammed All Jinnah advocated separate states for what was known as British India: one Hindu, one Moslem. His dream came true in August 1947, when the British pulled out. Pakistan was artificially separated into two regions: one in the east (now called Bangladesh) one in the west separated by more than 1,000 miles by the Indian subcontinent. Even the name of Pakistan is an acronym and comes from the first letters of Punjab, Afghanistan, Kashmir, India, Sind and the "tan" from Baluchistan.

From its inception, Pakistan was a nation in turmoil. Millions of refugees in the east who were Hindu fled to India: murder and mayhem erupted between the two religious groups who slaughtered each other with abandon. War then broke out with India over the regions of Kashmir and Jammu (MC opposition Mercury; ASC opposition Jupiter). Tensions escalated and General Ayub Khan seized power in a coup in October 1958 (MC opposition Venus sesquare Mars). His rule which lasted until March 1969 was rather benevolent for he corrected many things under his dictatorship (MC trine Uranus; ASC trine Neptune).

Dissatisfaction with being so far removed from the seat of power, East Pakistan revolted in March 1971 and by December had won its freedom (MC inconjunct Moon). From 1971 until 1977, Al Bhutto ruled Pakistan with an iron fist until he was ousted by General Zia (ASC sextile Venus). When the Soviets invaded Afghanistan, over more than three million refugees poured into Pakistan (ASC inconjunct Jupiter).

In November 1988, Bhutto's daughter, Benazir, became prime minister, the first female head of state in a Moslem nation (MC inconjunct Saturn and Pluto; ASC semi-square Saturn and Pluto). Bhutto was ousted on corruption charges in 1990 (MC inconjunct Venus; ASC conjunct Mars). Responding to Indian nuclear tests, Pakistan tested its own in May 1998 (MC square Uranus; ASC semi-square Sun). In the summer of 1999, tensions again erupted in Kashmir and soon after, martial law was instituted.

After the terrorist attacks in the U.S. in September 2001, Pakistan agreed to work with America to get rid of the Taliban in neighboring Afghanistan. Pakistan had previously supported the Taliban (MC sesquare Saturn and Pluto; ASC square Neptune) but the Bush administration was very persuasive.

Despite having the same planetary positions as India, there are a few notable differences. India has Gemini rising, Pakistan has Taurus rising with Jupiter opposite the ASC and the Sun, Venus, Saturn and Pluto squaring the eastern horizon. The Sun in Leo indicates the strongmen who have led this nation since independence (and one woman as well).

The Himalayas and the Hindu Kush occupy the northern borders of Pakistan. Desert flanks the fertile Indus river valley along which most of the populace resides. This land of 145 million people live in an area the size of England and France combined, slightly smaller than the state of Texas. Its original capital, Karachi, was founded in 1729. Government offices moved to Rawalpindi in 1959 and to Islamabad eight years later.

Karachi

Founded in 1729, Karachi is now one of the world's largest cities. Two centuries ago it was a small fishing village and didn't expand until the British built a railroad during the 1860s. It's still Pakistan's leading port even though it's no longer the capital, and hasn't been since 1959 when the government moved to Rawalpindi. Karachi now has the dubious distinction of being one of the most dangerous cities in Asia due to high unemployment and rampant poverty and disintegrating infrastructure.

Philippines
Republika Ng Pilipinas

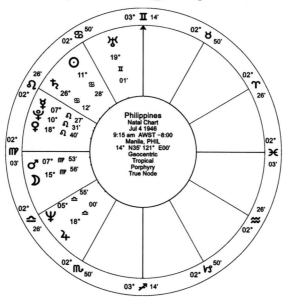

July 4, 1946, 9:15 a.m. ST, Manila
Source: Astrologer Serafin Lanot.

These islands were originally settled by people from the Malayan and Indonesian archipelagos. The Moslem invasion arrived in the 14th century but when Magellan claimed the region for Portugal in 1521, Christianity became the dominant religion. The Spanish conquered in 1583, making the Philippines the only major Spanish-speaking country in the Orient. It was ruled from Mexico. The independence movement began in 1896 under the aegis of a writer, Jose Rizal. Two years later during the Spanish-American War. Admiral Dewey destroyed the Spanish fleet in Manila harbor in May 1898. The U.S. took possession in December 1898 and paid Spain $20 million. The insurgents continued to fight American occupation until 1905, when William H. Taft became Governor of the Philippines. In 1935, these islands became a U.S. Commonwealth.

The Japanese launched a surprise attack on Manila in December 1941 and within the month occupied the capital. General MacArthur retreated to Luzon and eventually fled to Australia. The U.S. held Corregidor until May 1942. MacArthur returned in October 1944 and ousted the Japanese soon afterwards. America granted these islands their independence in July 1946.

Ferdinand Marcos was elected president in 1965 (MC semi-square Mercury; ASC square Uranus) and because of an impending Communist coup, declared martial law in September 1972 (MC semi-square Venus/Pluto). Martial law was lifted in January 1981 (MC sextile Mars; ASC conjunct Neptune). He then had the constitution amended making him president for life. Benigno Aquino, the opposition leader, was assassinated in August 1983, and his widow, Corazon Aquino, took up the banner against Marcos. She won the election in February 1986 and soon after, Marcos fled the country for Hawaii (MC conjunct Sun; ASC square Sun sextile Pluto).

Guerrillas continued to roam the country attempting to overthrow the government. Rebels bombed the Presidential Palace, took over military bases and TV stations in December 1989 (MC sextile Moon). The U.S. pulled out of Subic Bay in 1992 (ASC conjunct Jupiter sextile Venus), removing any American military presence in the country. A tentative cease-fire with rebels was signed in January 1994 (MC square Jupiter; ASC trine Uranus), but tensions remained high. Another treaty was signed in September 1996, creating an autonomous region on Mindanao where warfare had claimed more than 120,000 lives over two decades (MC semi-square Mars). Extremists in the southern part of the country called for a Holy War against the government in April 2001 (MC conjunct Saturn; ASC square Saturn).

The Philippines consist of 7,108 islands stretching over 1,100 miles in the western Pacific. Over 95 percent of the people live on only 11 islands, most of which are mountainous or volcanic in origin. The most fertile region lies in central Luzon. More than 80 million people live in an area the size of Italy or Arizona.

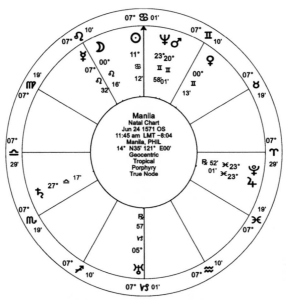

Source: Philippines astrologer Roman M. Uy says
11:25 a.m. Chart rectified.

Manila

Manila was founded by Legazpi on the site of an earlier village
in 1571 and it quickly became the largest and most powerful
stronghold in the Orient. Ships from Acapulco regularly plied their
wares across the Pacific, as the Philippines were allowed to trade
only with other Spanish colonies. An Audiencia (supreme court)
was founded in 1598 (MC semi-square Mars) and its University
established in 1619 (ASC trine Jupiter). In 1650, Dutch ships
raided the city during their conquest of the Far East (MC square
Neptune; ASC opposition Mars) and in 1762 the British occupied
Manila for two years (ASC sextile Neptune). By 1837, Manila had
been opened to foreign trade (MC trine Moon; ASC opposition
Uranus) five years after its new port was completed. Admiral
Dewey defeated the Spanish fleet in May 1898 (MC sextile Moon;
ASC square Venus) paving the way for American domination.

On December 8, 1941, the Japanese made a surprise attack on

Manila and the city fell three weeks later (MC semisquare Venus). During the last days of the war, the old city was in ruins and most of the city was one of desolation. In 1948, the government moved the capital to nearby Quezon City (ASC trine Mars) but Manila continues to be the lifeblood of the nation. A severe earthquake in 1968 caused extensive damage (MC inconjunct Uranus) and in 1975, Greater Manila was created, thus amalgamating 15 communities into one government.

Due to its fantastic growth in recent years, much of Manila appears to be quite modern. The most interesting sector is called Intramuros, the old Spanish district surrounded by 20 foot walls which run for more than two and a half miles. Much of this area was devastated after the war but efforts to preserve the old city have succeeded in retaining the heritage of colonial times. Manila was chartered as a city in 1574 and its Municipality was created on July 31, 1901. Most of the city lies on a low plain astride the bay and the entire region is prone to severe flooding during the monsoon season. Manila proper is home to two million people, but many more live in its surrounding area.

Qatar
Dawlat Qatar

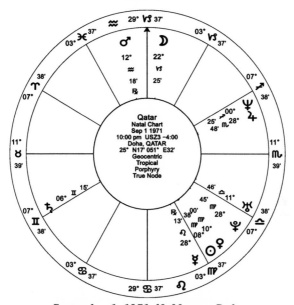

September 1, 1971, 10:00 p.m., Doha
Sources: The New York Times says "in the evening," while a
Kuwaiti radio broadcast at 7:00 p.m. GMT implies independence
had just been declared. Chart rectified.

For years, this region had been ruled by Bahrain. When Britain tried to muscle in and end Bahraini rule, they were themselves ousted by the Ottoman Turks in 1872 who then absorbed Qatar into their own empire. Britain finally assumed control in 1916 during World War I. Oil was discovered in 1940 along with huge deposits of natural gas.

Britain pulled out their troops in September 1971 and left Qatar to its own defenses. The Crown Prince ousted his father in 1995 (ASC square Sun) and women were allowed to vote in local elections by 1999 (MC square Jupiter inconjunct Pluto; ASC trine Uranus).

Qatar has about half a million people living in an area the size of Connecticut or half the size of Albania. It sits on a peninsula which juts into the Persian Gulf, a flat land of deserts and scarce vegetation. Only 45 percent of its people are Arabic; over a third are Pakistani or Indian.

Russia
Rossiyskaya Fedbratsiya

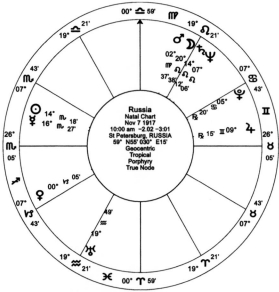

November 7, 1917, 10:00 a.m. LMT/DST
(6:59 a.m. GMT), St. Petersburg
Source: Lenin's Proclamation says 10:00 a.m.

The first Russian state was born September 20, 862 A.D. at Novgorod and named for its founder, Rurik. His dynasty died out in 1598, beginning a period called the Time of Troubles. Michael Romanov was named tsar in March 1613 and when he was crowned in Moscow on July 21, 1613 at 2:00 p.m. (per *The Romanovs* by Bruce Lincoln) his descendants would rule the largest nation on earth for the next 304 years. The last tsar, Nicholas II, abdicated due to massive losses during World War I which resulted in strikes, famine and starvation. A provisional government was formed in late February 1917 which ruled tenuously until Nikolai Lenin and his Bolsheviks took over the reins of power on November 7, 1917.

Lenin vowed to get Russia out of the war and in March 1918, he signed the Treaty of Brest-Litovsk which gave away much of Russia's territory (MC semi-square Mercury). Civil war broke out at the same time between the monarchists (Whites) and the Communists (Reds). The Soviet Union, which was a resurgence of the Russian Empire founded under Peter the Great and a government inside a government, was born in late December 1922 (MC square Pluto). Thirteen months later, Lenin died (MC sextile Neptune). Over the next few years, a power struggle developed between Stalin and Trotsky. Trotsky lost and was exiled to central Asia (ASC square Mars).

The various five-year plans, collectivization of farms and political purges made life in Russia during the Depression of the 1930s a virtual hell on earth. The purges began in December 1934 (MC trine Uranus; ASC trine Neptune).

Stalin signed a non-aggression pact with Hitler a few days before World War II began in September 1939 (ASC opposition Jupiter). Hitler went back on his word in June 1941 when he attacked Russia on his way to the Caspian. Stalin got his revenge, however, when his troops captured Berlin in April 1945 and soon after set up a puppet government (ASC trine Saturn). Due to a currency dispute, all communication and transportation was cut off in Berlin in June 1948, and to supply the city, the western allies began an airlift to keep the city alive (MC sextile Mars). Due to the Soviet ambassadors absence, the U.N. sent in troops to Korea in June 1950 when the Chinese Communists invaded the southern half of that country (MC trine Pluto). Three months before the Korean War ended in March 1953, Stalin passed away (MC square Neptune; ASC square progressed Mars). Two years later, Nikita Khrushchev became party chairman and began to assail Stalin's policies (MC inconjunct Jupiter; ASC trine Moon sextile Uranus).

The space race began in October 1957 when the USSR sent up its first space satellite, Sputnik (ASC sesquare Neptune). Two years after Fidel Castro took over the island of Cuba, the disastrous Bay of Pigs invasion took place when American troops tried to liberate that island (MC semisquare Venus). Khrushchev sent missiles to Cuba the following year and in October 1962, a standoff which could have resulted in nuclear war erupted when U.S. President Kennedy demanded those missiles be removed—or else (MC conjunct Mercury). Fortunately for the world, the Soviets removed the missiles and catastrophe was averted. Russia signed the SALT treaty in November 1969 and the world could now breathe a bit easier (ASC inconjunct progressed Jupiter).

Even though the Soviet Union held considerable sway and influence in eastern Europe, it invaded Afghanistan in December 1979 in its attempt to gain a route to warm water ports on the Indian Ocean (MC inconjunct Pluto; ASC sextile Sun inconjunct Saturn). The war would last until February 1989, when the Russians finally gave up. It was the Soviet Union's Vietnam.

Meanwhile, Mikhail Gorbachev had taken the reins of power in March 1985 (MC opposition Jupiter) and began to reform the system. By November 1989, the Berlin Wall came down and countries from the Baltic to the Black Sea said *adios* to more than four decades of Communist rule (ASC inconjunct Mars). After an abortive coup took place in August 1991, all of the other 14 constituent republics of the Soviet Union declared their independence. Gorbachev resigned his post on Christmas Day 1991 (ASC opposition Neptune trine Jupiter).

Boris Yeltsin had been elected president of Russia in June 1990. Sometimes he got too big for his britches and in September 1993, he disbanded the Duma, or parliament. The legislators threatened to impeach him (ASC square Sun oppostion Saturn). Beginning in December 1994, rebels in the southern district of Chechnya rose up in rebellion (ASC sextile Uranus) and Russian troops leveled its capital of Grozhny. Chechen rebels still spread their terrorist ways throughout western Russia to this day. In August 1998, Russia defaulted on its annual debt repayment (MC sesquare Neptune) and the economy which had exploded after the fall of the Soviet Union was now rife with corruption and mismanagement.

Yeltsin turned over the government to Vladimir Putin on December 31, 1999 (ASC trine Pluto) and within a year, private ownership of land was again permitted for the first time since the tsars ruled in Moscow (ASC square Jupiter).

Russia is the largest country on Earth, containing 11 percent of its land mass and spreading over 11 time zones. Only 20 percent of Russia lies in Europe, while 80 percent lies in Asia. This region is called Siberia. European Russia, however, has 80 percent of the population, while only 20 percent reside in Asia. Straddling two continents, the dividing lines are the Ural Mtns. and the Ural River, which flows into the Caspian. European Russia is a region of vast plains, wooded in the north and grassy further south. East of the Urals the land is frozen and marshy tundra towards the Arctic Ocean. On the border with Kazakhstan, Mongolia and China are the steppes and a forested region called the taiga.

Russia has the world's largest inland body of water, the Caspian Sea, as well as the world's deepest freshwater lake, Lake Baikal. The main rivers of Asian Russia are the Ob, Lena, Amur, Irtysh and Yenisei. Numerous volcanoes dot the region around the Kamchatka peninsula near Vladivostok on the Pacific Ocean.

Russia is a land of about 145 million people containing more than 100 nationalities. Its area of 6.6 million square miles is twice the size of the U.S. or Brazil.

Please Note: A more complete and detailed astrological and political history of Russia may be found in my book *The Horoscopes of Europe*, published by AFA.

Saudi Arabia
Al-Mamlakah Al-Arabiyah Al-Sahdiyah

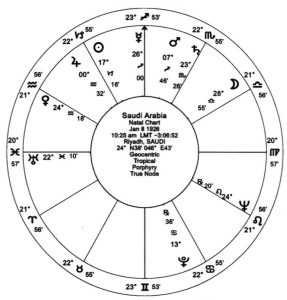

January 8, 1926, 10:25 a.m. LMT, Riyadh
Source: Encyclopedia Brittanica for the date; time rectified.

In ancient times, the northern part of this country was called Arabia Petraea, while the interior was known as Arabia Deserta. This region sits at the crossroads between Europe, Africa and Asia through which numerous caravans journeyed. It was here in Mecca, about 570 A.D., that the prophet, Mohammed, was born and where he died in 632 A.D. in Medina. During the next four centuries Arab armies spread Islam throughout northern Africa, Spain and the Middle East. In 1517, the region along the Red Sea became part of the vast Ottoman Empire.

In 1745, the Saud family conquered most of Arabia. They were followers of a strict, ultra-conservative, puritanical and fundamentalist sect called the Wahhabis. The first Saudi kingdom fell in 1818; the second kingdom was founded in 1824 and lasted until

1891. Ibn Saud began his conquest of the region in January 1902, when he attacked Riyadh and then made it his capital. During the next 24 years he conquered Hasa, Hijaz, Nedj and Asir, thus uniting several Arab tribes under this rule.

On January 8, 1926, Ibn Saud was declared king of Hejaz and sultan of Nejd and its dependencies. The new country was recognized first by the Soviet Union, then by Britain, France and Turkey. The U.S. recognized it in 1931. Just as the progressed MC entered Capricorn and the ASC moved into Aries and the Sun sextiled Saturn, the country was renamed the Kingdom of Saudi Arabia in September 1932, and Ibn Saud was crowned king on October 6.

Oil was discovered in 1938 and the first tanker left port in May 1939 (Sun conjunct Jupiter square Moon; ASC semi-square Venus sesquare Neptune and Saturn). The progressed ASC was also trine Mars, ruler of the second house of wealth. Like most of the Arab world, Saudi Arabia went to war against Israel in May 1948 (MC conjunct Sun; ASC sextile Venus trine Neptune inconjunct Saturn). Ibn Saud, founder of the country, died in November 1953 (MC sextile Uranus; ASC square Jupiter) and a power struggle began between two of his sons, Saud and Faisal, for the throne Saud won, but due to gross mismanagement, was forced to abdicate in March 1958 (ASC inconjunct Mars semi-square Uranus) and Faisal took over until December 1960, when Saud again took the throne (MC square Moon; ASC sesquare Mercury). Faisal took over again in April 1964, after the second abdication of his brother (Sun sextile Mercury; ASC sextile Pluto). Saudi Arabia decided to stay out of the war against Israel in June 1967 (Sun trine Moon sesquare Pluto; ASC trine Sun). The first five-year plan was implemented in 1970 to improve the country's infrastructure. In early 1973, OPEC raised oil prices and after the Arab-Israeli War of October 1973, oil prices quadrupled due to an oil embargo that sent economies around the world into panic (MC semisquare Mercury; ASC square Venus and Neptune opposition Saturn). Two years later in March 1975, King Faisal was assassinated by his nephew, and Khalid became king (MC inconjunct Pluto; ASC semi-square

Pluto). Meanwhile, Saudi Arabia was riding high economically and financially and started to spend on arms and aircraft, mostly from the U.S.

The year 1979 was a turbulent one for the Middle East. In February, the Ayatollah Kohmeini took over the government of Iran after the Shah left the country. Then Iranian militans took American hostages in November shortly before militants took over the Grand Mosque in Mecca. After a two-week siege which left 220 dead, the rebels surrendered (ASC sesquare Sun). Then at the end of December 1979, the Soviets invaded Afghanistan. Saudi Arabia had also severed relations with Egypt for signing a peace treaty with Israel. King Khalid died in June 1982 and was succeeded by his brother, Fahd (Sun trine Pluto sesquare Moon).

During the mid-1980s, oil prices began to fall. By 1986, the country was running a deficit as oil revenues were down by 85 percent and the price of a barrel of oil had shrunk by 75 percent. With massive armament spending, trying to fund Iraq against its war with Iran and also helping the Contras in Nicaragua, things looked pretty dire (Sun semi-square Jupiter; MC conjunct Venus opposition Neptune square Saturn; ASC opposition Mars, ruler of the second house of income).

In August 1990, Saddam Hussein of Iraq invaded tiny Kuwait and Saudi Arabia began to feel overly vulnerable (Sun conjunct Uranus; MC trine Moon sesquare Pluto; ASC sesquare Moon). The king allowed foreign troops to be stationed on Saudi soil and upped its oil production to account or the loss of Kuwaiti oil as most of the Kuwaiti wells were set ablaze by Hussein's troops during this short conflict. Internal dissent began to foment at this time over the quartering of foreign troops on Saudi soil. In 1992, the king formed the Consultative Council, an advisory group with no power to make laws on its own but a moderate step toward reform in this tradition-bound country (Sun square MC; MC semi-square Sun; ASC sesquare Jupiter). A bomb destroyed the Khobar Towers in Dhahran in June 1996 (ASC inconjunct Sun) shortly after King Fahd turned control of the government over to Prince Abdullah because of a stroke.

Saudi Arabia came under attack for fostering and funding terrorism after the attacks on American in September 2001 (ASC square Uranus inconjunct Saturn sextile Neptune trine Venus). Fifteen of the 19 hijackers who drove the planes into the World Trade Center in New York and the Pentagon in Washington DC were Saudi-born. Osama bin Laden, a Saudi who was "persona non grata" in his homeland claimed responsibility for the attacks. He formed Al Qaeda shortly after the war in Afghanistan where he worked as a freedom fighter with help from the CIA. The Saudis were also sympathetic to the PLO in its quest for a homeland. A U.S.-led coalition against Bin Laden invaded Afghanistan in October 2001, but the elusive terrorist could not be found. The U.S. invaded neighboring Iraq to oust Saddam Hussein in March 2003 (ASC opposition Mercury). Bombings in Riyadh that same year killed 52 people, most of them Moslems. The terrorists were probably educated inside Saudi Arabia to fight outside the country for Islam were now threatening the stability of the home country and its monarchy. King Fahd died in August 2005, and was succeeded by his brother, Abdullah (Sun trine Mars; MC trine Pluto sesquare Moon).

Saudi Arabia is the largest country in the Middle East. It occupies most of the world's largest peninsula, an area four times the size of France and three times as large as Texas. Home to 25 million people (10 percent foreign-born), it has a very high birth-rate, which makes for high unemployment among young males. Most of the country is an inhospitable and forbidding desert, but there is a narrow strip along the coasts that is fit for agriculture. Petroleum and natural gas are the main resources and exports, and Saudi Arabia has 25 percent of the world's known oil reserves. However, at the current rate of consumption, those reserves will run out in half a century unless new fields are discovered.

Saudi Arabia is an absolute monarchy run like a corporation with members of the royal family sitting on the board. It has no constitution or bill of rights, no congress or parliament and no suffrage. The country is held together by pledges of loyalty and obedience to the king from leaders of local tribes, just as in the Middle

Ages where a lord ruled over a fiefdom. The monarch is shown by the Sun in Capricorn in the tenth house opposition Pluto. This is an aspect of strength, determination and persistence to keep the status quo with much power and control spent on resisting undesirable change. Capricorn is tradition-minded but ambitious, but slow to alter time-honored customs and belief systems. The Sun opposition Pluto detests others telling them what to do and in this country, it's the Saudi way or the highway. This opposition also points to internal conflict between the monarchy and the people it governs who want reform and change.

The Moon in Libra in the eighth house could point to the tremendous wealth this country has beneath its soil, not to mention the lavish spending sprees that the wealthy go on every now and then. This aspect is generous, open-handed and often wasteful; nobody has ever stated that the Saudis were miserly or penny-pinchers. The Moon in Libra often wavers from one viewpoint to another, giving the appearance of seriously considering altering the status quo. But in the end, things rarely change diplomatically or politically as the Moon is at the end of Libra and about to enter the intransigent sign of Scorpio. Meanwhile, there's that smiley face that obscures one's true feelings in the hopes of not alienating one's partners. This aspect of the Moon in the eighth house could, also point to the high birthrate along with the fact that Arab men are allowed to take up to four wives at one time.

Mercury, as ruler of the DSC and IC, points to the fact that some of Saudi Arabia's enemies are homegrown, especially students and budding intellectuals. Mercury's aspects are generally benign with sextiles to the Moon and Venus, a good indication of salesmanship if not double-talk. Mercury also trines Neptune, ruler of the ASC, so the rulers of the ASC and DSC are in harmony. But Mercury also squares Uranus on the ASC so the more educated the Saudis become, the more they question things and the more they will rebel. This aspect might also point to the relative lack of a free press or media. Mercury is the lower octave of Uranus, so grade-school education conflicts with more universal truths. When Saudis leave the country on business or vacation, they often do things they're not allowed to do in their homeland, like kick up their heels and have a good time. This Mercury squaring Uranus is often an innovative aspect, reforming and questioning everything in sight. But Uranus is retrograde, so change comes slowly, if at all, but not without considerable stress and turmoil.

Venus in Aquarius is involved in a T-square to Neptune and Saturn, probably the most difficult aspect in this chart. To me, this points to the dichotomy of Saudi males who on one hand worship and adore their women but at the same time try to control their every action. It could also indicate some internal inferiority with women or just the fact that in the old days, marriages were arranged for financial or dynastic reasons and love seldom entered the picture. Venus governs the third house of basic education and its opposition to Neptune and square to Saturn bodes warning when the natives begin thinking for themselves, especially in religious matters. Is the basic philosophy of the Saudi brand of Islam, Wahhabism, compatible with the modern age or will their brand of religion stultify creative thought and innovation? Venus in the twelfth house could also point to the isolation of women, doubly so as it opposes Neptune, the nominal ruler of the twelfth house. Neptune rules the veil behind most women must remain elusive and hidden.

Saturn occupies the ninth house of religion and philosophy. The Koran is the basis for this country's legal structure and its application is called the Sharia. Saturn is a strict planet with little room for frills, serious argument or interpretation. The Wahhabi belief system harks back to the early days of Islam centuries ago and the imams and religious scholars see little need for change or reform. Saturn in the ninth house also indicates the strict morality and harsh punishments often meted out to criminals, especially crimes of a sexual nature, like adultery or homosexuality. Saturn, as ruler of the Sun in Capricorn, could indicate that underneath Saudi Arabia is a land based on the teachings of Mohammed as outlined in the Koran and that this country is probably a theocracy, just like Iran.

Note also that Mars in Sagittarius occupies the ninth house.

This points to the rapid and militaristic spread of Islam in the centuries following the death of Mohammed. Despite the martial nature of this aspect, Islam gave the world a new viewpoint on astronomy, mathematics, science, the arts, literature and architecture. Europe was in the Dark Ages and Islam was a beacon of light for those who thirsted for knowledge and inspiration. The Moslem world experienced a Renaissance centuries before Europe came out of the closet, especially in the cosmopolitan and sophisticated cities like Cairo and Baghdad. Mars in this ninth house could also point to the schism that developed between the Sunni and Shia branches of Islam, as Sagittarius is a double-bodied sign. When Neptune, then Uranus and now Pluto crossed the ninth house cusp, Islam began a resurgence politically and philosophically. The militancy of some Moslems inside Saudi Arabia has been carried to foreign countries and often resulted in acts of terrorism against Jews and Christians, not to mention other Moslems. Car bombings and suicide bombers willing to risk their own lives for eternal glory in the afterlife are today a constant threat to world peace and understanding. Militants are probably revolting against what they deem as errant Moslems in foreign countries where laxity is more prevalent than it is allowed to be inside Saudi Arabia where repression, suppression and adherence to convention and tradition are respected.

Using a 30-degree dial, one notes that Mars in the religious sign of Sagittarius in the ninth house of philosophy aspects both Saturn and Uranus. Talk about extremes, one planet extolling virtue, tradition and, the status quo from times long gone, the other planet worshiping innovation, revolution and change. This dichotomy exists inside Saudi Arabia today, mainly between the young students and the religious clerics. Taken together, this puts considerable stress and strain on Mars which often fights for both extremes. One should also note that on the 30-degree dial that the Moon aspects Pluto, ruler of the ninth house of law and religious freedom. Not only does the Sun oppose Pluto in this chart but the Moon negatively aspects Pluto as well. Talk about living at home with one's parents after college and still being told what to do with little freedom for individuality or true freedom of expression.

119

Saudi Arabia has many challenges ahead in the coming years, especially as Pluto crosses the Midheaven and squares the Ascendant. Things are changing under the surface and could erupt at breakneck speed when the genie opens the bottle. Growing agitation and antagonism of the young against high unemployment, internal terrorist activities, financial damage control against over-spending by the monarchy, economic reform, educational expansion, the establishment of human rights, freedom of the press, the rights of women and religious freedom are matters this country will have to deal with if it is to survive as a monarchy. Change seems to be something Saudi Arabia resists, even though it has Uranus rising. But note that Uranus is retrograde which makes it reactionary, stubborn and resistant to change. It comes across as more of a fascist dictator than a liberator and often thinks it knows what's best for the people as a society and to hell with individuality and personal freedom. One should remember that both Hitler and Franklin D. Roosevelt had Uranus rising—so draw your own conclusions.

Mecca

Located 40 miles east of the port city of Jedda, Mecca is Islam's most holy city. Mohammed was born here in 570 A.D. and Muslims are required to make a pilgrimage here at least once in their lives. Mohammed fled the city to Medina to avoid religious persecution. The most famous sight in the city is the Kaaba which contains the Black Stone supposedly given to Abraham by the archangel Gabriel. Non-Moslems are forbidden to enter the city upon threat of penalties and deportation.

Riyadh

Located in the center of the country, it's one of the most isolated and least-known capitals, but one of the most modern. The old walls weren't torn down untile the 1950s and most foreign embassies didn't even bother to move here until the 1970s. Riyadh is the center of the Wahhabi sect of Islam which is extremely puritanical and very conventional.

City of Singapore

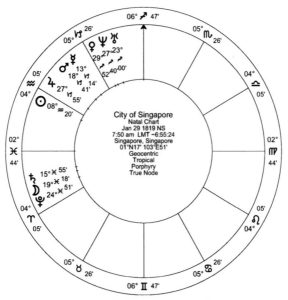

January 29, 1819, 7:50 a.m., Singapore
Source: Singapore Tourist Office for the 1819 date; Book of World
Horoscopes by Nicholas Campion.

The first settlers on this island were Sumatrans who landed here about 1000 A.D. A town called Timasek was founded in 1250 but destroyed by the Javanese in 1365. Due to the fighting spirit of the natives, the city was called "Singapura," or Lion City, after the courage of its citizens. During the 18th century, Singapore was part of the Dutch colony of Johore, ruled by a Sultan, and it was from this Sultan that Stamford Raffles bought the island on January 29, 1819 thus beginning the modern history of this city-state. In 1826, Singapore was joined to Malacca and Penang to form the Straits Settlement and in 1867, it was made a separate Crown Colony administered from British India (ASC trine Venus).

With the opening of the Suez Canal in 1869, the fortunes of Singapore were greatly increased (MC conjunct Jupiter). It soon became the largest port in southeast Asia as it was located in the main

121

Country of Singapore

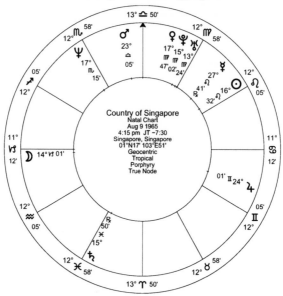

August 9, 1965, 4:15 p.m.
Source: Book of World Horoscopes by Nicholas Campion

route from Europe to the Far East. Due to its strategic location, it became a major naval base for the Allies during World War II and was thus imperative for the Japanese in their desire for supremacy in the region. Japanese troops attacked in February 1942 (MC sextile Sun; ASC inconjunct Sun), but did little damage to the city. Singapore became a separate colony in 1946 and achieved internal self-role in 1959. After its union with Malaysia in 1963 (MC trine Pluto), tensions arose between the numerous Chinese against their Malayan overlords. It was then decided to secede from the union and form an independent city-state which was done on August 9, 1965 (ASC trine Neptune opposition Jupiter). The largest airport in southeast Asia was opened in 1981.

Singapore is the fourth-largest port in the world and probably the most strategically-situated community in the Orient, shown by the MC in Sagittarius. Its economy gives its citizens the second-highest standard of living in the Orient after Japan shown by the ruler of the second house, Mars sextile the Moon, Saturn and Pluto. Singapore is the financial, retail, commercial and industrial center of the region, outranked only by Hong Kong. Taxes are levied against those who have more than two children, illustrated by the Moon as ruler of the fifth house conjunct Saturn and Pluto. Stiff license fees restrict the number of autos that may enter the central business district. There's also a stiff penalty for litterbugs, so don't throw away those cigarette wrappers onto the street. Appearances count for much in Singapore; those who have long hair are forced to get it cut and women who show too much thigh or leg are requested to don more appropriate attire. Note Venus in Sagittarius conjunct Neptune, ruler of the ASC, and both of them square Pluto, ruler of the ninth house of legislation. This tiny city-state also has a hard-line approach to crime, and those who deal in drugs, prostitution or gang violence are given a mandatory death sentence. Note that Uranus, which conjuncts the ruler of the ASC and rules the twelfth, is also square Pluto. Singapore seems to be run along the ideals of its leader, Lee Kwan Yew, and the situation seems to be working even if its citizens are denied several freedoms generally given to residents of more westernizes countries. Singapore is the entrepreneur's dream city where money can be made quickly and with relative ease. It's also one of the cleanest and most efficiently run places on earth where little seems to be out of place and everything runs like clockwork, so typical of those planets in Capricorn with Saturn rising.

Singapore is situated on an island containing 225 square miles and has two and a half million people. Over 75 percent of the population is Chinese and the literacy rate of 85 percent is one of the highest in the world. The main industry is shipbuilding but its main exports are electronic equipment. Singapore is the world's third-largest oil refining center and the banking hub of southeast Asia.

Sri Lanka
Sri Lanka Prajatantrika
Samajavadi Janarajaya

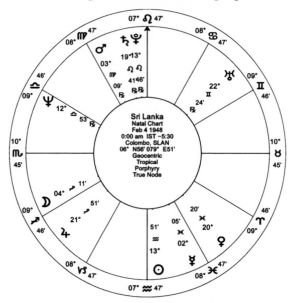

February 4, 1948, 12:00 a.m., Colombo
Source: The New York Times says midnight.

Twenty years after the birth of the Buddha (543 B.C.) tribes from India subdued the native Veddahs. Sixty years later, the first Sinhalese kingdom was founded. Arab traders arrived in Ceylon during the 12th century to be followed by the Portuguese in 1505. The Dutch arrived in 1658 and were themselves ousted by the British in 1796. Ceylon holds the honor of being the first Asian country to grant women the vote back in 1931. The British finally pulled out in early 1948 when they granted Ceylon its freedom within the British Commonwealth.

In 1959, Prime Minister Bandanaraike was assassinated (MC conjunct Saturn; ASC inconjunct Uranus). The following year, his wife took the reins of power and became the first female head of

124

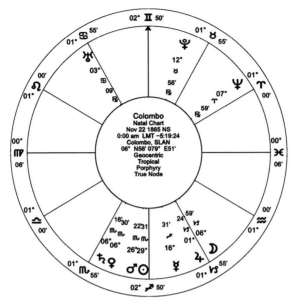

November 22, 1865, 12:00 a.m.
Source: National Archives

state in the Orient (MC inconjunct Venus). She surrounded herself with Marxists, expropriated American and British oil firms and instituted several socialized enterprises, most of which failed. Meanwhile, the economy was going down the toilet at record pace. Student riots in 1971 prompted a state of emergency which lasted for six years (ASC square Mercury). Ceylon became the Republic of Sri Lanka in May 1972 and left the British Commonwealth (ASC square Mars conjunct Moon).

During the 1980s, riots broke out between the native Sinhalese and the Tamils who are Hindu. Tensions over the past two decades have resulted in more than 60,000 being killed and some 12,000 have simply disappeared. In late December 2004, the eastern shore of Sri Lanka was hit by a massive tsunami which was the result of a catastrophic earthquake off the coast of Sumatra (MC semi-square Saturn; ASC sesquare Saturn/Pluto). Thousands were drowned and international aid poured in from around the world.

Sri Lanka is an island nation lying off the southeast coast of India. The northern half is flat while the south is hilly. Over two-thirds of the population of 20 million are Buddhists and live in an area the size of Holland and Belgium combined. The capital is Colombo which was founded by Arab traders in the 8th century.

Colombo

Situated on the west coast, Colombo is the chief port of the country. Founded by Arab traders, it was captured by the Portuguese in 1517 and by the Dutch in 1658. The British conquered the city in 1796 and a new harbor was built a few decades later after railways were introduced. Plans are underway to move the capital to the city of Kotte sometime in the near future.

Syria
Al Jumhuriyah Al-Arabiyah Al-Suriyah

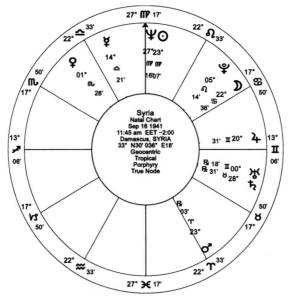

September 16, 1941, 11:45 a.m. EET, Damascas
Sources: The New York Times and The Times of London
state "during the day." Chart rectified.

During ancient times, Syria was part of the Assyrian, Babylonian, Persian empires. The Greeks invaded in 330 B.C. under Alexander the Great and the Romans took over in 64 B.C. The Byzantines ruled for three and a half centuries until the Arabs invaded in 637 A.D. The Ottoman Turks came in 1516 and held sway until April 1920 when the French gained the mandate to rule over the region. The original territory was divided between Syria and Lebanon.

Independence was proclaimed in September 1941 but the French were in no hurry to depart. It wasn't until April 1946 that full independence was achieved. Along with its neighbors, Syria invaded Israel in May 1948 (MC sextile Pluto). To expand Arab influence in the Middle East, Syria joined with Egypt and Yemen and formed the United Arab Republic in February 1958 (MC semi-square Saturn conjunct Mercury). The UAR disbanded in September 1961 (ASC square Neptune).

In March 1963, the militant Baath party seized power (ASC sextile Venus inconjunct Uranus). During the Six-Day War with Israel in June 1967, Syria lost the Golan Heights (MC sextile Moon) which overlooked the Sea of Galilee. In October 1973, Syria again invaded Israel (MC inconjunct Saturn and Uranus).

When the Civil War in Lebanon erupted in 1976, Syria stepped in as mediator, and it has remained there to this day, much to the dislike of the Lebanese. (MC conjunct Venus). By 1986, Britain broke relations with Syria and limited sanctions were imposed by the European Union. Like many nations, they felt that Syria was fostering and promoting terrorism in Arab lands (MC semi-square Neptune).

Syria, however, fought on the U.S. side against Iraq during the Gulf War in 1991 (ASC trine Saturn and Neptune). After ruling Syria for three decades, Hafez al Assad died in June 2000 and was succeeded by his son who got 97 percent of the vote (MC conjunct Sun and Neptune). After turmoil in neighboring Lebanon, Syrian troops and government officials were asked to leave the country (MC opposition Uranus semi-square Mercury; ASC trine Mercury sesquare Neptune).

Syria is a land of 17 million people living in an area the size of Austria and Portugal combined. From the small coastline on the Mediterranean, plains and lowlands rise to mountains and then desert. Syria is the source of the Euphrates River, one of the longest bodies of water in the Middle East.

Damascas

Situated 55 miles east of the Mediterranean Sea, it's one of the oldest continuously-inhabited places on earth. Mentioned about 2500 B.C., it was known as the town of Shem, named after the son of Noah, six centuries later. During its centuries of history, it's been ruled by every empire from the Egyptians to the French. Located at an elevation of 2,265 feet, Damascas is a major rail crossroads. Its most famous sight is the Great Mosque, built in 708 AD, which contains the tomb of Saladin.

Taiwan
Chung-hua Min-kuo

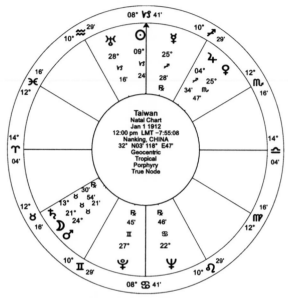

January 1, 1912, noon LMT, Nanking, China
Source: Autobiography of Sun Yat-Sen.

Immigration to this island began in the 7th century when refugees from the mainland began to colonize what was then called Formosa. The Portuguese arrived at the end of the 15th century but the Dutch held sway from 1620 until 1662. The Manchus conquered Taiwan in 1683 until the Japanese took over in 1895 after the Sino-Japanese War. Japanese rule ended with their defeat in World War II in August 1945 (MC square Saturn).

With the fall of the Kuomintang to the armies of Mao Tse-tung in 1949, General Chiang Kai-shek moved the government of Nationalist China to Taiwan in December 1949 (MC square Moon/Saturn; ASC opposition Jupiter sesquare Sun/Uranus). Two million refugees fled from the mainland to escape the Communist takeover. During 1955, the offshore islands of Matsu and Quemoy

130

were shelled by the Communists (MC inconjunct Neptune square Moon; ASC inconjunct Sun). Despite objections from the U.S., Taiwan was expelled from the U.N. in 1972 in order to admit the People's Republic of China (MC sextile Sun; ASC conjunct Pluto inconjunct Uranus semi-square Saturn).

Chiang Kai-shek died in 1976 (MC sextile Saturn sesquare Uranus), having led the Nationalist government for several decades. Formal relations with the U.S. were severed in 1978 and two years later, Taiwan lost its membership in the World Bank and the IMF (ASC inconjunct Jupiter).

In 1987, martial law was lifted after 38 years (MC trine Venus sextile Mars square Mercury; ASC opposition Sun) and the following year, travel to mainland China was eased (MC square Pluto; ASC sesquare Venus). By 1991, emergency rule ended after 43 years (MC sextile Uranus semi-square Saturn; ASC sextile Saturn). Nationalist Party rule ended in March 2000 (ASC sesquare Jupiter).

Taiwan has 2.3 million people living in an area the size of Portugal or Indiana. Despite its lack of political influence in the world arena, Taiwan enjoys the third-highest standard of living in the Orient, after Japan and Singapore. Due to its liberal laws, its products are sold the world over and its prices remarkably inexpensive. One world of caution, however; there are no copyright laws in Taiwan which makes this the biggest publishing center in Asia. The capital is Taipei, founded in 1795.

Taipei

Taipei is located 18 miles from the port city of Keelung. Founded as a market town in 1795, it was made the seat of prefecture in 1875 (MC conjunct Mercury) and the capital of Formosa 20 years later (MC opposition Jupiter). As Taiwan had become part of Japan that year, its name was changed to Taihoku, (ASC conjunct Neptune).

When Communists took over the mainland in 1949, the Nationalist government under Chiang Kai-shek moved its offices to this

131

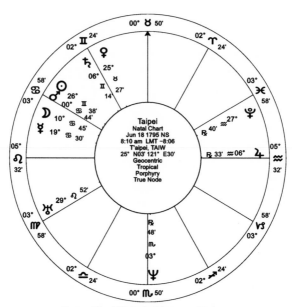

June 18, 1795, 8:10 a.m., Taiwan
Source: National Central Library; no time mentioned.

city in December (MC square Mars). In July 1967, Taipei was created as a special municipality. The city occupies 105 square miles and has about two million inhabitants.

Tajikistan
Jumhurii Tojikistan

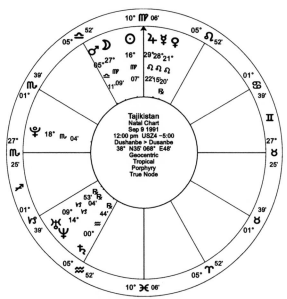

September 9, 1991, noon (7:00 a.m. GMT)
Source: No time given in any source.

During the 6th century B.C., this region was settled by the Persians. Arab armies arrived in the 7th century A.D. and the Uzbeks ruled from the 15th to 18th centuries. Russians took over in the 19th century and made this region part of the Soviet Union in 1929. Independence came in 1991.

In January 1993, a pro-Communist regime came to power (progressed ASC square Mercury). This prompted a civil war between the government and Islamic rebels between 1992 and 1997 (progressed ASC square Jupiter). Islamic political parties were legalized in September 1999, but by 2001, armed gangs were mining the border with Uzbekistan (progressed ASC sextile Mars).

This region the size of England or Illinois has six million people living in one of the most mountainous regions on earth. Much of

133

the country is more than 10,000 feet in elevation, with peaks of the Tien Shan, Pamir or Trans-Alai ranges. The highest point is Communism Peak (elev. 24,590 ft.) the highest point in the old Soviet Union.

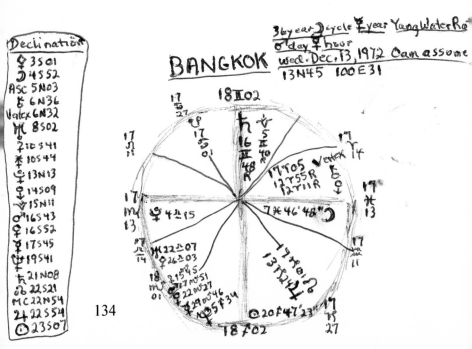

134

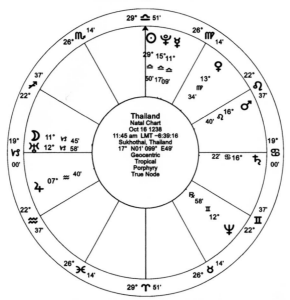

By D. K. Wyatt - Thailand, A Short History p.35-38 Bangkok 2003 gives Oct. 2, 1238 Chiang Saen 20N16 100E56 birth of King Mangrai (last quarter Moon 10:56am LMT)

Thailand
Muang Thai

Thailand
Natal Chart
Oct 16 1238
11:45 am LMT −6:39:16
Sukhothai, Thailand
17° N01' 099° E49'
Geocentric
Tropical
Porphyry
True Node

October 16, 1238, noon, Sukkothai
Source: Los Angeles Herald-Examiner;
no time mentioned; noon presumed.

By the 35th century B.C., this region began to use bronze. Ancestors of the Thais migrated here from Yunan province in China during the 11th century and a kingdom was founded in 1238 which still rules the country. Thailand, or Siam, is the only country in the Orient never to have been conquered by a foreign power. Thailand means "land of the free."

In 1767, the region was united by the Ghakkri dynasty who moved the capital to the newly-created city of Krung Thep, also known as Bangkok (MC square Moon, Uranus and Neptune; ASC conjunct Saturn). During the latter half of the 19th century, strides were made to modernize Siam, trade began to flourish and slavery was abolished.

135

In June 1932, a coup forced the King to give up absolute power and a constitution was framed before the end of the year (MC = Sun/Mars). During World War II, Japanese troops briefly occupied Thailand (MC semi-square Mars) and after the Vietnam War, thousands of refugees fled here from the Communists. In 1976, a bloody coup brought the military to power (MC square Jupiter; ASC square Sun/Pluto).

During the 1990s, AIDS and HIV began to ravage the country, possibly due to a history of relaxed sexuality which prompted sex tours from more repressive societies (MC semi-square Mercury; ASC opposition Mars inconjunct Saturn). Over 750,000 people in Thailand are now infected with the AIDS virus. The Asian financial meltdown in 1997 prompted Thailand to ask for $15 billion in loans to keep its economy from going under (MC semi-square Moon and Uranus; ASC trine Pluto). In late December 2004, a massive tsunami generated by a catastrophic earthquake in Sumatra swept through resort areas in western Thailand killing thousands (MC semi-square Pluto; ASC semisquare Mercury).

Thailand is a nation of 61 million people in an area the size of Spain or twice the size of Oregon. The northern part is heavily forested; the south has jungles and rain forests. Through the center of the country flows the Chao Phraya river, the most fertile region of Thailand. The capital is Bangkok which was founded in 1782.

Looking at the chart we note that the Sun in Libra, the sign of peace, could well indicate why this country has had no foreign domination in its history. The Moon in Capricorn conjunct Uranus and Saturn in the seventh might account for this Oriental phenomenon as well. Modernization began in the 19th century when Pluto crossed the bottom of the chart and finished when Pluto trined the Sun just before World War I. Uranus rising indicates its name, the land of the free. Venus in Virgo in the eighth house trine the Moon and Uranus and sextile Saturn might indicate the sexual freedom of the Thai people, but its square to Neptune in the fifth house of love and romance warns of dangers if one is not careful due to the high incidence of HIV and AIDS.

Lahari
Ayamsa
9°♓11'03"

Yang
Water Tiger

April 16
1782
6:54am LMT
t day th.

gryphonastrology.com

New Moon Eclipse April 13, 1782 ♀ day ♃ hour

17 26♎36

♊♃ ┼
♊ 26♈36

☋16♈22
☉☽ 22♈54

Bangkok

In 1769, Thon Buri was made capital of Siam after the city of Ayutthaya was destroyed by Burmese invaders. In April 1782, the new capital of Krung Thep (Bangkok) was inaugurated by King Rama 1, across the river from Thon Buri. During the early 19th century, Bangkok was known as the "Venice of the East" due to its homes being built on stilts to protect them from periodic flooding and its numerous canals. In 1851, King Rama IV, opened the city to foreign trade (MC sextile Mars) and three decades later, the old city walls were torn down.

By the 1920s, many canals had been filled in or paved over to facilitate automobile traffic. Locks then had to be constructed to control the ever-present problem of flooding during the monsoon season, shown by the Moon near the IC opposition Pluto at the MC and both square the Sun, ruler of the fourth house.

Declination
♀ 0N04
☿ 0S37
♆ 0S58
♅ 5S53
☋ 6S22
☉ 11N49
♂ 13N23
ASC 16N26
MC 18S43
♄ 22S19
♃ 22S59
♂ 23N02
☽ 23N43
♀ 23S50
☽ 24N34

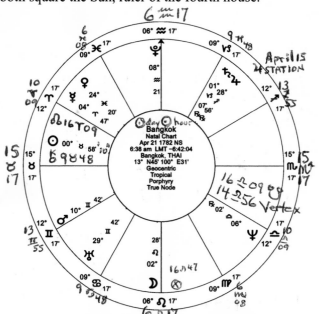

April 21, 1782, 6:38 a.m., Bangkok
Source: Col. Chong Plaeg Banchong, a Thai astrologer, ☉ day ♀ hour
says 6:54 a.m. Chart rectified 6:54am LMT (6:42:06)
♀ 8♎21
MC 10♎14
☉ 0♎58'49"
☋ 9♈48
ASC 137 19
♀
36
☽ 2♌36'13"
Vertex 16♎24
☋ 16♈08

bi centenary celebration April 6, 1982
celebrations April 14-21, 1982

From late 1941 until 1945, Bangkok was occupied by the Japanese (MC inconjunct Pluto) but the government never fell to the invaders. Metropolitan Bangkok was formed in 1971 (MC opposition Pluto) uniting Krung Thep and Thon Buri for the first time in history.

Located on the banks of the Chao Phraya river some 25 miles from the Gulf of Siam, Bangkok is one of the most cosmopolitan cities in the Orient. The main sights in the city are the Grand Palace which was completed in 1785 which covers an area of one square mile. Surrounding the palace are numerous wats, or temples, for which this city is so famous. Wat Pho has a golden Buddha, Wat Phyakeo has an Emerald Buddha and the Wat Arun is the tallest point in the city reaching a height of 245 feet.

The most pressing problem facing Bangkok today is that much of the city is sinking, some parts are already below sea level. It's predicted that Bangkok will be entirely below sea level within 50 years, requiring higher and higher dikes to be constructed to keep out the river. Bangkok occupies 110 square miles and is home to five million inhabitants in its metropolitan area.

Turkey
Turkiye Cumhuriyeti

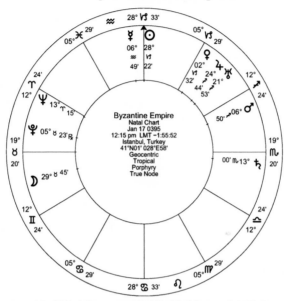

January 17, 395 A.D., noon LAT, 12:15 p.m. LMT, Istanbul
Source: Encyclopedia Brittanica for the date. Noon assumed.

Byzantine Empire

By the 20th century B.C., Asia Minor had become the seat of the vast Hittite empire which lasted until the Assyrians conquered it in the 14th century B.C. By 687 B.C., Anatolia had become part of the Persian empire under Cyrus the Great and Darius. Greeks came in 334 B.C. when Alexander the Great of Macedon conquered the area on his way to the Orient. By the 1st century AD, most of Anatolia was part of the Roman Empire.

Emperor Constantine decided to build a new capital for the Roman Empire on the site of the ancient Greek city of Byzantium. The foundation stone was laid in November 326 A.D. and this new city which he named after himself, called Constantinople, was dedicated in May 330 A.D. As the Roman Empire was simply too vast and unwieldy, it was divided on January 17, 395 A.D., and thus was the Byzantine Empire founded which would last for more than a thousand years until it was overrun by the Ottomans.

Moslems invaded Turkey in the 7th century and converted its churches into mosques. Anatolia was taken by the Seljuk Turks in 1038 and the Byzantines surrendered to them in 1071. Meanwhile, there was dissent inside the Roman Church, and those differences resulted in the Great Schism of July 1054 which permanently separated the Roman Catholic Church from the Eastern Orthodox whose influence extended throughout the Balkans into Russia and Anatolia.

In 1204, Crusaders attacked Constantinople on their way to the Holy Land, looting and pillaging everything in sight. Shortly after, Mongols invaded from the steppes of Asia. Inside Turkey, a man named Osman was beginning to conquer lands previously held by the Byzantines by the end of the 13th century.

Ottoman Empire

The Ottomans captured the city of Bursa on April 6, 1326 and made it their capital (MC semisquare Mercury; ASC sesquare Pluto). The capital was moved to Edirne in 1361 (MC conjunct Jupiter). Turks fought the Serbs at the battle of Kosovo in June 1389 (MC square Sun) and four years later Bulgaria became part of their emerging empire (ASC opposition Mercury semisquare Uranus). The Byzantine Empire finally surrendered to the Ottomans on May 29, 1453, when the city of Constantinople surrendered (MC square Jupiter; ASC opposition Moon). No longer would Europe be the bastion of Christianity as Muslims were now taking over the Balkans.

Greece fell in 1460 (ASC trine Pluto), Bosnia in 1463 (MC opposition Mercury), Albania in 1468 (ASC square Mercury) and Wallachia (modern Romania) in 1476. In 1526, the Ottomans captured Hungary and laid siege to Vienna (MC trine Mercury), threatening the Hapsburg domains. The Ottoman naval fleet was defeated at Lepanto in October 1571, and Ottoman power waned

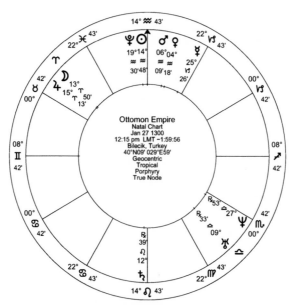

April 6, 1326, noon LAT, noon LMT, Bursa
Source: The Ottoman Centuries by Kinross and other
historical manuscripts.

afterwards. The Turks laid siege to Vienna in July 1683, and would have captured that city had not troops arrived from Poland at the last minute (ASC semisquare Saturn trine Neptune). Upon their departure the Ottomans left behind sacks of a beverage called coffee, new to Europeans, and the rest, as they say, is history. The Ottomans were finally ousted from Hungary in 1699 (MC semisquare Venus; ASC square Uranus).

Catherine the Great, Tsarina of Russia, was also seeking to expand her empire so she went to war with the Turks in 1774 (ASC inconjunct Mars) and the Ottomans lost the Crimea. The Serbs revolted in 1804, and the Greeks declared their independence in April 1821 (ASC opposition Jupiter). Nine years later, in 1830, their freedom was guaranteed (MC square Neptune).

The Crimean War began in April 1853 against Russia (MC opposition Pluto). With British and French assistance, Turkey regained the Crimea, and Russia lost its right of passage through the Bosporous from the Black Sea to the Mediterranean. A Constitution was framed in 1876 and Turkey got its first Parliament, but the following year things returned to normal and the Constitution was torn up (MC sesquare Mercury; ASC sesquare Moon). The Russo-Turkish War of 1877 over Bulgaria was occurring at the same time that the Romanians were declaring their independence. The Treaty of Berlin in July 1878 granted freedom to Serbia, Bulgaria and Romania (MC semisquare Neptune; ASC sesquare Moon/Jupiter). Only tiny Albania remained an Ottoman province in Europe.

A student uprising in 1908 restored the Constitution (MC sextile Saturn; ASC semisquare Mars). War against Italy erupted in 1911 (MC trine Sun) and in November 1912, Albania broke loose from Ottoman control (ASC semisquare Mars/Saturn). Meanwhile, the First Balkan War broke out in October 1912 against its former European provinces, and the Second Balkan War erupted in June 1913.

World War I began in August 1914 with Turkey on the Axis side with Germany, Austria and Bulgaria against the rest of Europe (MC trine Pluto). The Turks defended the peninsula of Gallipoli in April 1915 against the Allies, many of whom were from Australia and New Zealand. Deportation of Armenians in eastern Turkey also began in April 1915, which many believe was an attempt to annihilate the Armenians. The British began to free many Middle Eastern countries under Ottoman control in 1916, including Lawrence of Arabia (ASC sesquare Saturn sextile Neptune).

The Turks were still fighting when the Germans signed the armistice in November 1918. Kemal Attaturk resisted any attempt at Allied occupation of his homeland, much more so after the Greeks invaded Smyrna in September 1919 (ASC semisquare Sun). In August 1920, Ataturk became president of Turkey and the Greeks were driven out of Smyrna and other coastal communities (MC square Mercury). Ataturk separated the religious sector (Caliphate) and the political sector (Sultanate) in November 1922. The

Treaty of Lausanne was signed in 1923, ending Turkey's involvement in World War I. Turkey became a republic in October 1923 (MC conjunct Neptune; ASC semisquare Pluto).

Turkey

With the proclamation of the Turkish Republic on October 29, 1923, Kemal Ataturk became its first leader. The new capital was Ankara, the Caliphate was abolished in 1924 and the Greeks and Bulgarians repatriated (progressed MC trine Venus; progressed ASC square Mars sesquare Jupiter). Over the next few years, Ataturk completely redesigned Turkish life in his attempt to bring his country into the modern world (progressed ASC conjunct Pluto). Ataturk made the Latin alphabet requisite for writing Turkish, he banned the fez and veil and prohibited religious political parties from having any voice in the government. Like Lenin in Russia, Ataturk pushed Turkey full-force into the 20th century. He also banned polygamy and proclaimed that all religious beliefs would be tolerated and Islam would not become the state religion. Ataturk died in November 1938 (progressed Sun square Neptune; transiting Jupiter square Jupiter; Saturn square Pluto; Pluto sesquare MC).

When World War II began in September 1939, Turkey decided to remain neutral, a wise decision considering its disaster in the previous war (progressed Sun semi-square Mars; progressed MC sesquare Venus; transiting Jupiter inconjunct Sun). In order to become a charter member of the U.N., however, Turkey was forced to declare war on Germany, which it did in February 1945, but Turkey saw no action on the battlefield (progressed Sun sesquare Pluto; progressed MC opposition Mars; progressed ASC trine Jupiter square Mercury and Saturn). In 1950, Turkey joined NATO (progressed MC square Pluto; progressed ASC sesquare Uranus).

Riots broke out on Cyprus in 1955. Britain ruled the island which had a large Greek population with a sizeable Turkish minority (progressed Sun sextile Mars; progressed MC inconjunct Venus). Britain granted Cyprus its independence in August 1960 and a military coup executed the old leaders of Turkey (progressed

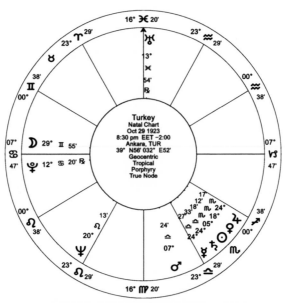

October 29, 1923, 8:30 p.m. EET, Ankara
Source: Emergence of Modern Turkey by Lewis says 8:30 p.m.

Sun inconjunct Pluto; progressed ASC square Sun; transiting Saturn opposition Pluto; Uranus conjunct Neptune; Pluto sextile Sun; Neptune trine ASC). Martial law was in effect for one year (progressed Sun square Uranus; progressed MC opposition Saturn and Mercury). In 1964, Turkey became an associate member of the European Union (progressed ASC sextile Mars).

After the removal of Archbishop Makarios of Cyprus in July 1974, Turkey invaded that island and gained control of 40 percent of its territory (progressed MC inconjunct Mars; transiting Saturn conjunct Pluto/ASC; Uranus conjunct Mercury/Saturn; Neptune sextile Mars; Pluto semi-square Neptune). Turkish Cypriots established a separate state on the northern part of Cyprus, and Turkey took over most of the U.S. bases on that island (progressed ASC square Venus).

Turkey was placed under martial law in 1978 (progressed MC sextile Pluto; progressed ASC conjunct Neptune) and a military

144

government took the helm in September 1980 (transiting Uranus sesquare ASC). The press was censored and more than 20,000 Turks became political prisoners (progressed Sun semi-square Venus; progressed ASC semi-square Mars; progressed MC sextile Uranus). Martial law was rescinded in 1984 (progressed Sun square Mars; progressed MC opposition Venus; progressed ASC square Jupiter sextile Mercury and Saturn).

In June 1993, Kurdish rebels demanded an independent state in the eastern part of Turkey, and Turkey also got its first female prime minister (progressed MC semi-square Pluto; transiting Mars opposition Jupiter; Jupiter conjunct Sun; Saturn trine Pluto). In June 1997, the pro-Islamic government was forced to resign under pressure from the military (progressed Sun inconjunct Neptune; transiting Mars square Moon; Uranus inconjunct ASC). The Kurdish rebellion ceased after February 1999, when its leader, Ocalan, was captured and sentenced to death (transiting Mars trine ASC; Jupiter square Moon). In 2001, Turkey went through a major financial crisis and the IMF stepped in. The Civil Code was expanded for more rights for women at the same time (progressed Sun sextile Jupiter; progressed ASC semi-square Mercury and Saturn).

In order for Turkey to eventually join the European Union, it will have to adhere more strictly to human rights protocols and to eliminate torturing of suspects and criminals. Turkey will also have to reform the military which has staged three coups in recent years and still dominates the government. Journalists will also have to be freed in a country which has only limited right of free speech and the press. And lastly, the question of its occupation of northern Cyprus will have to be addressed. Turkey made a few reforms in mid-2003 by increasing freedoms for the minority Kurdish population which can now broadcast their own language over radio and TV channels. Kurds will also be allowed to give their children Kurdish names and another law was repealed which gave reduced sentences to those who committed "honor crimes," i.e., the killing of women who are accused of bringing shame to their families.

Located at the juncture of Europe and Asia, Turkey is bordered by the Black Sea on the north, the Aegean Sea on the west and the Mediterranean Sea on the south. Continentally, it's separated by the Bosporous, the Sea of Marmara and the Dardanelles (Hellespont). The coastline is 4,471 miles long. The European part of Turkey is called Thrace (9,121 square miles) while its Asian part is called Anatolia, or Asia Minor, a wide and treeless plateau surrounded by mountains. The highest point is Mt. Ararat (elev. 16,945 ft.). The population is more than 66 million, with 80 percent Turkish and 19 percent Kurdish; 99 percent are Moslem. With 301,382 square miles, the country is larger than Texas and 50 percent larger than France, 34 percent arable and 74 percent urban. Main exports are cotton, tobacco, citrus, olives and carpets. Main resources are antimony, coal, chromium, mercury and copper. Unfortunately, the largest cash crop is illegal drugs like hashish and heroin.

Istanbul

Founded in 659 B.C. by Byzas, the city known as Byzantium grew to be the largest city in the eastern Mediterranean by the time Emperor Constantine decided to make it capital of the Roman Empire in 324 A.D. Named after himself, the foundation stone was laid during the hour of the Crab on November 4, 328 and dedicated on May 11, 330 at 4:00 p.m. In 381, this city became the seat of Patricarch (progressed Ascendant conjunct Neptune) and when the Roman Empire split in two in 395, Constantinople assumed the role of capital (ASC square Uranus). In 413, walls were built surrounding the city on the Golden Horn and in 439, a seawall was constructed. By 537, the fabled Cathedral of St. Sophia was completed, but five years later a plague wiped out 20 percent of the populace (ASC square Sun) as did the Arabs in 675 (MC semi-square Moon) who lost their fleet. Bulgarians tried to conquer the city in 813, as did the Russians three times over the next two centuries.

With the Great Schism in the Church in 1054 (ASC trine Mercury), Constantinople became headquarters for the Eastern Orthodox Church, the Second Rome. In 1097, the First Crusade passed

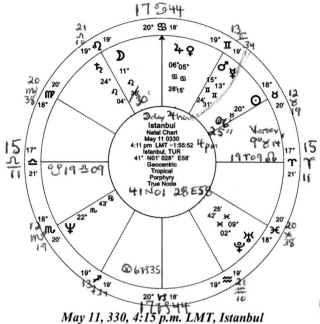

May 11, 330, 4:15 p.m. LMT, Istanbul
Sources: Istanbul University Library gives the date and time.
Encyclopedia Brittanica gave time of 4:00 p.m. Chart rectified.

through this city on its way to the Holy Land and in 1204, Crusaders sacked and pillaged this glorious port (MC square Uranus, ASC square Sun). By 1302, the district of Galata became a walled fortress.

The chief turning point in the history of modern Constantinople occurred May 29, 1453, when the siege by the Ottoman Turks ended (ASC trine Pluto), thus making this a Moslem city and capital of their empire. Santa Sophia was turned into a mosque and Christians left for friendlier climes. Under Suleiman the Magnificent (1520-66), Constantinople rose to new heights of power and glory due to the establishment of the Caliphate (ASC trine Saturn). Over the next four centuries life was relatively peaceful in this city of nearly a million people. In 1838, the first bridge across the Golden Horn was completed and by 1885, water and sewage lines were completed. In 1912, electric lights finally lighted this fabled city that spans two continents.

147

During World War I, Constantinople was blockaded by the Allies (MC opposition Sun; ASC semi-square Pluto). In 1920, the Sultanate was abolished with the collapse of the Ottoman Empire. The capital was moved to Ankara in 1923 and the Caliphate eliminated the following year (ASC inconjunct Jupiter). On March 28, 1930, Constantinople was renamed Istanbul, which means "downtown" in Greek (MC square Uranus; ASC square Sun). In 1973, the first suspension bridge across the Bosporus was opened (MC trine Sun; ASC sextile Jupiter) thus linking the European side of this city to that on the Asian continent.

Istanbul is located on the Bosporus, the narrow strait which links the Black Sea (19 miles to the north) to the Sea of Marmara, which eventually empties into the Aegean Sea after passing through the Dardanelles. Over its long history, this city has been witness to more than 50 earthquakes and 60 fires, most of its important structures were left intact. Towering over Istanbul are three mosques: Hagia Sophia, the Blue Mosque and the Suleimaniye. At the tip of the Golden Horn lies the Topkapi Palace containing the famous Seraglio of the Sultans.

Despite the majority of Istanbul lying on the European continent, this city has a decided Oriental flavor. Natives love to sit at the numerous coffee houses sipping the beverage they introduced to the Europeans three centuries ago when they besieged Vienna. Like most eastern cities, Istanbul has a terrible traffic problem as most of its streets are little wider than alleys. The Galata Bridge is the most heavily used in the world and over the din may be heard the muezzins calling the faithful to prayer four times a day. If ever a city deserved to be called "the Crossroads of the World," Istanbul should be placed close to the top of that list. The Old City has nine square miles, while the New City which spans the Bosporus is 98 square miles in area. The population is close to three and a half million, most of them Turks but also with a sizeable Greek minority.

Ankara

Capital and second-largest city of Turkey, Ankara is located in the center of the Anatolian plateau 220 miles east of Istanbul.

Founded in the 8th century B.C. as Angora by the Phrygians, it was the capital of the Roman province of Galatia. Capital of Turkey only since 1923, it has grown from a town of 30,000 to a metropolis 100 times that size.

A huge monument to the founder of modern Turkey, Kemal Ataturk, towers over the city. A few structures still remain from Roman times which contrast sharply with the very modern appearance of Ankara. The Archaeological Museum is a treasure trove of Hittite artifacts from a kingdom that ruled this region milleniums ago. Ankara is also famous for its leatherwork and its mohair, which comes from the Angora goat for which this city is named.

Turkmenistan

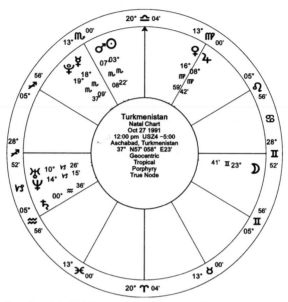

October 27, 1991, noon (7:00 a.m. GMT) in Ashgabat
Source: No time given in any source.

Around the first millennium, Turkic tribes arrived from central Asia. Two centuries later, the Mongols invaded the region, one century before Islam came to the region. By 1881, it became part of Russian Turkestan. Union with the Soviet Union took place in 1924 and independence from that Union was achieved in 1991. It has been ruled by Niyazov since that time around whom a cult of personality (shades of Stalin) has developed. He rules as a virtual dictator, has little use for basic rights and freedoms we take for granted here in America like freedom of speech, religion or assembly.

Turkmenistan is a country of 6 million people living in an area the size of Spain. Over 80 percent of the country is occupied by the Kara Kum desert. The Caspian Sea is on Turkmenistan's western border. This country has extensive oil and natural gas reserves.

150

United Arab Emirates
Al-Imarat Al-Arabiyah Al-Muttahidah

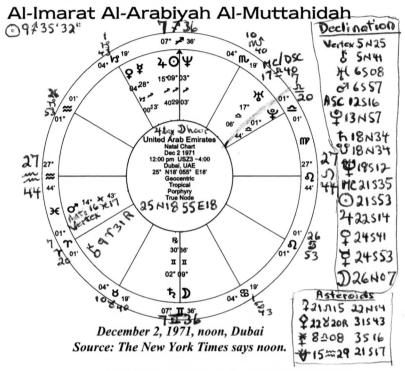

December 2, 1971, noon, Dubai
Source: The New York Times says noon.

Britain signed a peace treaty with seven sheikdoms in 1820, thus giving Britain control over defense and foreign relations. The region was known as the Trucial Coast. The British pulled out in 1971.

Nearly three million people live in an area the size of Indiana or Portugal. A narrow, flat coastal plain gives way shortly to a region of sand dunes. The UAE has the world's second-highest GDP (after Qatar) due to numerous oilfields and its petrochemical industry. International banking is also prominent. The seven sheikdoms are: Abu Dhabi, Dubai, Sharjah, Ajman, Umm al Qaywayn, Ras al Khaymah and Al Fujayrah.

151

Uzbekistan
Uzbekiston Respublikasi

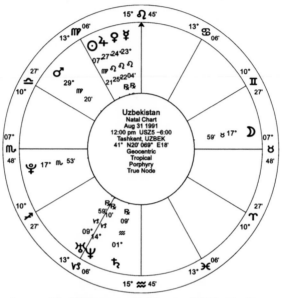

August 31, 1991, noon (6:00 a.m. GMT), Tashkent
Source: No time given in any newspaper.

In the 6th century A.D., Turkic people arrived from central Asia. A century later, Arab legions arrived and brought Islam to the region. During the 14th century, Samarkand became the capital of Tamerlane's empire; this was a century after the region had been overrun by the Mongols. Khanates ruled the region by the 16th century but with the coming of the Russians in the 19th century, they were abolished. Uzbekistan became part of the Soviet Union in 1924 and upon achieving independence in 1991, the government was headed by former Communists. Over the next decade, this country battled terrorism and Islamic militants intent on forming a theocracy.

This land of 25 million people occupies an area the size of Spain. Plains occupy the western part while deserts occupy most

152

of the rest. The Amu Darya and Syr rivers drain into the Aral Sea which over the past four decades has shrunk to half its size due to massive irrigation projects.

North Vietnam

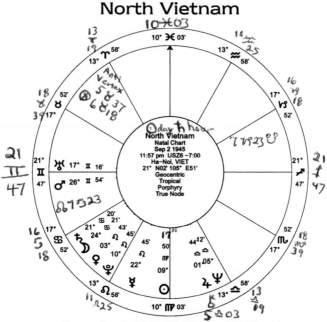

September 2, 1945, 11:57 p.m. ST, Hanoi
Source: Local Vietnamese newspapers.

From 111 B.C. until 939 A.D., what is now North Vietnam was under Chinese control. Another kingdom in the south, called Champa, was founded about the same time. The two regions were united in 1471, but two centuries later, it was again divided into Tonkin in the north and Cochin in the south. France took over both regions in 1859 and formed Indo-China. The French then divided this area into three districts: Tonkin (north), Annam (center) and Cochin (south). The entire region was made a French protectorate in 1884. French Indo-China added Cambodia in 1887 and Laos in 1893.

The Japanese occupied Vietnam during World War II and on the same day the Japanese surrendered, Ho Chi Minh declared the independence of Vietnam. Emperor Bao Dai fled to the south and internal strife continued for another nine years. French troops invaded the Chinese sector of Haiphong in November 1946 (MC inconjunct Pluto; ASC sextile Mercury) thus beginning three decades of warfare. The French made this region part of the French Union in March 1949 (ASC conjunct Mars semi-square Pluto) but couldn't control matters. After the horrible defeat at Dienbienphu in May 1954, the French thought it wise to depart. On July 21, 1954, Vietnam was divided at the 17th parallel (MC sesquare Venus). In 1964, Soviet and Chinese arms arrive to aid in the escalating conflict (ASC semi-square Mercury). The U.S. also started bombing North Vietnam at this time as well. After the fall of South Vietnam in April 1975, the entire country came under Communist rule. In July 1976, both nations were united (MC inconjunct Sun).

South Vietnam

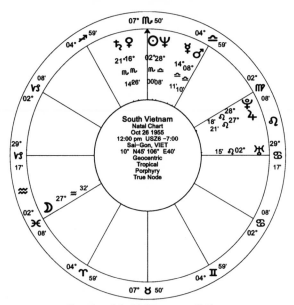

October 26, 1955, noon, Saigon
Source: The Times of London.

South Vietnam came into being as a republic under Ngo Dinh Diem. A coup backed by the U.S. in November 1963 ousted Diem who was then assassinated (MC conjunct Venus; progressed ASC square natal MC). As war became imminent, U.S. President Johnson sent in troops after American ships were shelled in the Gulf of Tonkin in August 1964 (ASC trine Mars). Over the next nine years, more than 500,000 American troops would be sent to this region with 12 percent of them dying to save this country from Communism. A peace treaty was signed in January 1973 (MC square Jupiter and Mercury/Mars; ASC trine Mars/Neptune). Americans finally pulled out after the fall of Saigon at the end of April 1975 (MC square Moon and Pluto). North and South Vietnam were formally united in July 1976 (MC semi-square Mercury; ASC square Saturn). The country which was founded with 29 Capricorn on the ASC officially ended when the progressed MC stood at 29 Scorpio.

Vietnam
Gonq Hoa Xa Hoi Ghu Nghia Viet Nam

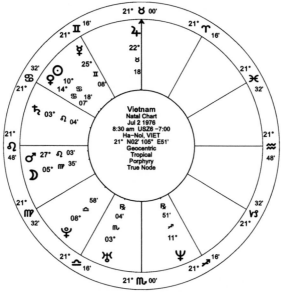

July 2, 1976, 8:30 a.m. ST, Hanoi
Source: The New York Times says 8:30 a.m.

Vietnam was born with Jupiter at the MC square the ASC. After three decades of fighting, it was now time to rebuild this shattered nation. During the U.S. involvement, 200,000 Vietnamese soldiers were killed, 58,000 Americans lost their lives and more than one million Vietnamese civilians were slaughtered. More than six and a half million refugees had also fled to neighboring countries. Hanoi was to be the new capital and Saigon was renamed Ho Chi Minh City.

In 1979, Vietnam invaded Cambodia during that country's war of genocide and annihilation and set up a puppet government (MC semi-square Sun). Towns along the Chinese border were obliterated. The U.S. refused to establish diplomatic relations with Vietnam until it returned 2,500 soldiers still listed as missing in action.

Some 10,000 children were allowed to leave Vietnam to be with their fathers in America. Many Vietnamese became boat people in their quest for freedom but many others fleeing Vietnam were forced to live in refugee camps in neighboring countries.

Beginning in 1987, reforms were made to reduce the centralization of the economy and many old-timers were removed from the government (MC inconjunct Uranus; ASC conjunct Moon/Mars). In February 1994, the U.S. ended a 19-year embargo and restored diplomatic relations with Vietnam in July 1995 (MC opposition Neptune). U.S. President Clinton signed a trade deal with Vietnam in July 2000 (ASC sextile Venus).

Vietnam is a country of 80 million people living in an area the size of Finland or New Mexico. The north is hilly and mountainous while the south is fertile due to the Mekong River. About 25 percent of the country is arable but most of it is jungle. The capital of Hanoi was founded about 600 A.D. on the banks of the Red River some 80 miles from the China Sea. The largest city is Ho Chi Minh City (aka Saigon) which has more than five million residents.

Hanoi

Situated on an arm of the Red River 80 miles from the Gulf of Tonkin, it became capital of Vietnam in 1010 A.D. and known as Thang Long. It was renamed Hanoi in 1831. The French laid out the modern city when it was the capital of French Indo-China from 1887 to 1945. Heavily bombed during the Vietnam War, tourists have recently discovered the city and its many charms.

Saigon (Ho Chi Minh City)

Situated on the river Saigon 50 miles from the coast, the city grew up as a trading center for plantation owners along the fertile Mekong river. During the Vietnam War, thousands of people from the countryside fled to Saigon, which at the war's end was renamed to honor the President of Communist North Vietnam. Even though it's no longer a capital city, it retains the distinction of being the largest city in the country.

North Yemen

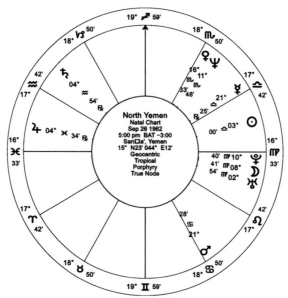

September 26, 1962, 5:00 p.m. BGT, Sana
Source: The New York Times says 5:00 p.m.

In ancient times, this region was known as the Kingdom of Saba or Sheba, whose Queen made a famous visit to King Solomon of Israel and produced a son named Menelik from whom the Ethiopian emperors were descended. During the 7th century A.D., Arabs invaded and brought Islam. The Ottoman Turks came in 1517 and ruled for the next four centuries. After World War I, Yemen attained independence as a monarchy.

A Republic was formed during a military coup in September 1962 at the moment when Mars was inconjunct the MC, Another coup occurred in June 1974 (MC square Sun sextile Jupiter trine Uranus). A peace treaty with Marxist South Yemen was signed in March 1979 (MC trine Moon; ASC inconjunct Pluto). In May 1990, both Yemens were united (MC semi-square Jupiter; ASC sesquare Pluto).

South Yemen

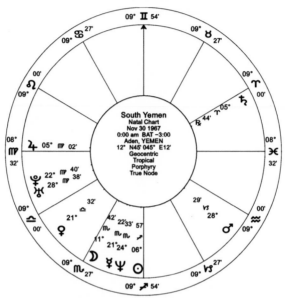

November 30, 1967, 12:00 a.m., Aden
Source: The New York Times says midnight.

In 1839, this region then called Aden became a British Crown Colony. After the Suez Canal was opened 30 years later, Aden became an important, stopping off point for those on the road to the riches of India. Aden received its independence from Great Britain in November 1967 and then became the Arab world's first Marxist state. Note that Venus, ruler of the ninth house of philosophy, sits at the midpoint of the Sun and Jupiter. Soviet troops arrived in 1979 (MC trine Venus square Pluto), a decade after refugees had fled to North Yemen or Saudi Arabia. Both Yemens were united in May 1990.

Yemen
Al-Jumhiriyah Al-Yamaniyah

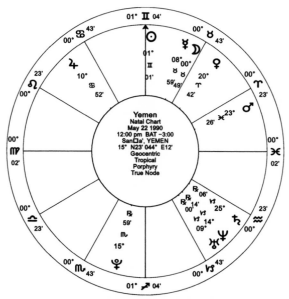

May 22, 1990, noon BGT, Sana
Source: International Herald Tribune says noon.

In 1993, multi-party elections were held with women running as candidates (MC semi-square Venus). Unfortunately, the following year, a brief civil war erupted as the southern half of the country wished to secede (ASC sesquare Venus). In the harbor of Aden in October 2000, the USS Cole was bombed, probably by terrorists influenced by Osama Bin Laden and his terrorist network of Al Qaeda (MC sesquare Saturn; ASC trine Uranus). The U.S. accused Yemen of being sympathetic to the terrorists.

Yemen lies at the southwest corner of the Arabian peninsula. Its 18 million people live in an area the size of Spain. A sandy coastal strip yields to fertile mountains in the interior; on the other side is the vast Rub-al-Khali desert.

161

Australia, New Zealand and the Pacific

American Samoa

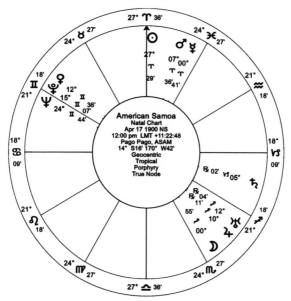

April 17, 1900, noon, Pago Pago
Source: U.S. Department of Interior, noon presumed.

American Samoa was discovered in 1722 by Jacob Roggeveen. The French explorer, Bougainville visited in 1768. During the 1830s, American whalers and missionaries began to arrive. A triparite agreement between the U.S., Britain and Germany was signed in 1899 to administer this South Seas paradise but the U.S. took complete control in 1900.

American Samoa was under the jurisdiction of the U.S. Navy until 1951 (MC conjunct Pluto; ASC square Venus and Uranus). It then became the responsibility of the Department of the Interior. In January 1978, American Samoa elected their own Governor for the first time (MC inconjunct Uranus; ASC trine Pluto).

Samoa is the southernmost possession of the U.S., about 2,300 miles southwest of Hawaii. Its seven islands are mostly bush or mountains. The population is 60,000 and lives in an area the size of

Brooklyn, New York or Washington DC. The capital is Pago Pago where it seems to rain all the time.

Australia

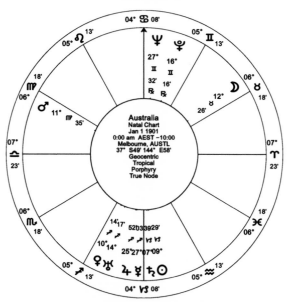

January 1, 1901, 12:00 a.m., Melbourne
Source: Federation of Australian Astrologers. Proclamation took
place in Sydney at 1:00 p.m. according to The Times of London and
other local newspapers.

Australia was discovered by Captain Cook in 1770, who claimed the region for Great Britain. Due to overcrowding in English jails and prisons, convicts could no longer be shipped off to America, which had won its independence in 1783. Parliament decided to rid England of its undesirables and ship them off to this remote land. The First Fleet left England in May 1787 and landed at Botany Bay (just south of Sydney) in January 1788. Life was harsh for the convicts and a matter of sheer survival as crops wouldn't grow and supply ships were few and far between. Convict transportation continued until 1840 and was completely phased out by 1868. Nearly 160,000 convicts were shipped to Australia, the most hardened being eventually sent to distant Norfolk Island in the Pacific.

Gold was discovered in May 1851 in the state of Victoria and in Western Australia in 1892. State boundaries were in place by the end of 1859, and on the first day of the 20th century, Australia was born.

Australia was still, however, part of the British Empire so when Britain went to war in August 1914, Australia sent its troops to the front (ASC sesquare Pluto). During the battle of Gallipoli in April 1915, soldiers from both Australia and New Zealand (the Anzacs) suffered a huge defeat. When the war ended in November 1918, Australia suffered a 69 percent casualty rate, more than any other Allied nation during World War I (ASC sextile Saturn).

Australia was particularly hit hard during the Depression which began in late 1929 (ASC semi-square Sun/Saturn). It had barely recovered when World War II began in August 1939 (MC square Moon semi-square Neptune) and Australia again sent its troops to aid the "mother country." Japanese planes bombed Darwin in 1942 (MC sextile Pluto) and then the tide started to turn. With the end of the war in August 1945 (progressed Sun sextile Jupiter; ASC square Mars inconjunct Moon), thousands of immigrants flowed into this country from Europe.

When the Korean War broke out in June 1950 (MC trine Jupiter; ASC opposition Pluto), Australia again sent what many said were "the most fightin' men in the world." When the Vietnam war broke out in 1963 (MC sextile Sun/Saturn; ASC opposition Neptune), it was a 12-year stint until the fall of Saigon. Aborigines were given citizenship and the right to vote in 1967 (progressed Sun square Pluto; MC sextile Moon). Immigration reform ending the "whites only" system was ended in 1973 (ASC conjunct Saturn) and since then, thousands of Asians have been admitted into the country.

When the progressed ASC was conjunct the Sun and the progressed Sun square Jupiter in 1975, a constitutional crisis occurred when the elected prime minister, Gough Whitlam, was confronted by heretofore quiet conservatives. Whitlam's tenure was quite progressive. The draft was abolished, troops were removed from Vietnam, Communist China was recognized, and the social welfare system was overhauled and plans were made for universal healthcare. Government support for the arts also increased and the Australian film industry began to take off. Then it hit the fan: oil prices went up in 1973 and inflation and unemployment reared their ugly heads. Whitlam's foe was Malcolm Fraser who used his power to deny the government funding for the above-mentioned projects. Whitlam refused to resign so the governor-general, Sir John Kerr, acting as the official representative of the Queen of England, dismissed Whitlam and called for an election. After Fraser took over, he dismantled many of Whitlam's programs and Australia sank into a conservative torpor, even while its currency was being devalued right and left.

Australia celebrated its bicentennial in 1988 and hosted the 2000 Summer Olympics. Earlier that year, Australians had voted not to become a Republic, thus getting out from under the wing of the British Commonwealth (MC trine Uranus; ASC sesquare Moon inconjunct Neptune). For a people so famous for being independent and freedom-loving, this was an odd decision until you remember that this nation was born under a Sun/Saturn conjunction with the Moon in traditional Taurus which abhors change.

Australia is a nation of about 20 million people living on the world's largest island, the sixth largest country in area. Australia also governs Norfolk Island, Christmas Island, the Cocos Islands and the Australian Antarctic Territory. Over 90 percent of its people are European, seven percent are Asian and about one percent are Aborigines. This is the driest continent on earth (after Antarctica) and most of the outback, or bush, receives scant rainfall and is a desert. The eastern coast and the island of Tasmania are where most of the people live. The Great Dividing Range runs down the eastern coast of Australia and reaches heights of more than 7,000 feet. The main rivers are the Murray and Darling.

Australia's main exports are beef, lamb, wool and wheat. Only six percent of the country is arable and suitable for agriculture. The chief mineral resources are bauxite, diamonds, gold, iron ore and nickel. Australia also mines most of the opals found in jewelry stores.

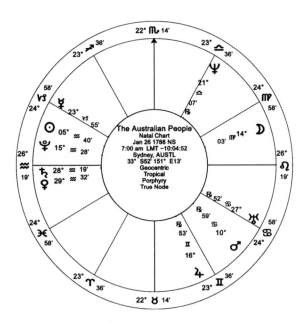

The Australian People
Natal Chart
Jan 26 1788 NS
7:00 am LMT −10:04:52
Sydney, AUSTL
33° S52' 151° E13'
Geocentric
Tropical
Porphyry
True Node

The Australian People

To ascertain the true characteristics of the Australian people, or Aussies, the early convict heritage must always be taken into consideration. Jupiter sesquisquare the Sun in the twelfth house combined with Mars sesquisquare the Ascendant produced people who were rebels at heart and highly distrustful of any authority figure. True to the nature of Aquarius, Australia has become the most egalitarian nation with almost complete absences of great wealth or poverty.

Saturn rising points to those early years of hardship when life was simply a matter of survival with the supply ships few and far between. Crops brought by the settlers didn't grow in the sandy soil, and the climate was totally alien to the first European inhabitants. Despite these obstacles, and the inbred rebelliousness, Australia has become one of the most conservative and cautious nations on Earth. Most Aussies are middle class and, true to the nature of Saturn, desire to preserve the status quo.

Saturn conjuncts Venus, so proving if one had the patience,

benefits would eventually follow. Venus in Aquarius makes the Aussies cordial people, often overly-polite and ingratiating. A strong moral and ethical strain has also produced a sense of propriety and decorum, just like that of the mother country.

This conjunction, however, might account for the inherent fear and dislike of close female companionship. Men would rather endure a drought, bush fire or famine than spend their free time with the ladies. Mateship is vital to the survival of the species in this arid land where distances are vast and communication to limited to bush pilots and ham radios. Despite advances made in recent years, most Australian women still take a back seat to their menfolk. Note that six planets are in masculine fire and air signs.

Despite this Saturnine influence, Aussies don't really take life all that seriously. Note that Mercury in Capricorn (which often produces a rare sense of humor) is opposite Uranus and square Neptune. There's a strong self-effacing attitude which occasionally surfaces with the tendency to deprecate native accomplishments. Mercury's aspects also account for the distinct and unique lingo, called Strine, which is filled with many colorful colloquialism and phrases.

Neptune ruling the second house accounts for the lack of competitiveness in the economic arena. Aussies don't like to work overtime or take second jobs. Neptune square the ruler of the eighth house causes taxes on extra effort to be disproportionately high; Aussies are a rather spartan people, with possession being limited to the basic necessities of life. Prices for goods and services are considerably higher than they should be, but remember that Australia has fewer people than the state of California. A sizable portion of the national income is spent on welfare and subsidies.

Mars governs the third house, so travel, freedom of movement and the ability to pioneer and explore are of vital concern. As Mars is also concerned with accidents and injuries, it comes as no surprise that Australia has one of the highest highway death tolls in the world. Recent steps have been taken to curb excessive drinking. The highways become slaughterhouses on weekends, especially in the outback where roads are straight and the settlement sparse. Mars rules speed, and this one arena concerning transportation is a national disgrace. It shows up in the national horoscope as well.

Venus rules the fourth house, so Aussies desire to own their own home, complete with outdoor barbecue and a small garden. Taurus is fixed and compact, however, so it should come as no surprise that over 90 percent of the people live in urban areas. Jupiter in the fourth points to the vast open spaces in the interior, called the bush or outback. Most of this region to uninhabitable due to the lack of water. Note that Jupiter is square the Moon. Irrigation, however, could solve this problem (see trines of Jupiter).

Mars in the fifth points to Australia's reputation as a nation of "sport fanatics." Natives pack the stadiums, race tracks and beaches en masse, and Aussies are probably the healthiest-looking people on Earth, despite the high incidence of skin cancer. Aussies will gamble on most anything, and games of chance are taken quite seriously, with Mercury in Capricorn ruling the fifth house. This is truly one arena in which the Aussies excel, for their competitive spirit knows no bounds where sporting events are concerned. Aussies are also known as the fiercest fighting men on Earth, despite the overwhelming disaster at Gallipoli during World War I.

With the Moon ruling the sixth house and square Jupiter, along with Uranus in the sixth house opposition Mercury and square Neptune, Australia has had severe problems with its extremely powerful labor unions. Life periodically comes to a standstill when the rails or mails go on strike, often on holiday weekends.

The Virgo Moon indicates an over-concern with health matters and disease. Planes are always sprayed before allowed to land from foreign countries, and animal quarantine laws are among the most stringent. Despite Virgo's reputation for neatness, the Aussies aren't the most tidy people. Their streets and highways are just as littered as those in America.

The Sun in Aquarius rules the seventh house, making Aussies among the most friendly, open, informal and easy-going people on this planet. Candid and often blunt to the extreme, they either like you or not. They take you at face value, having little gullibility or skepticism. There's a refreshing lack of sophistication, phoniness or pretense in the typical Aussie. They're an often naive and simplistic people who prefer to be forthright and direct in speech. Saturn's co-rulership of Aquarius, combined with Saturn rising, also makes for the typical British reserve, especially with the Sun in the twelfth house. The much talked-about inferiority complex of the nation might be traced to this signature, along with the Moon in Virgo. But Australia surely has many accomplishments about which to brag, especially in the music and entertainment fields. Names like Joan Sutherland, Helen Reddy, the Bee Gees, Olivia Newton-John, Mel Gibson, and Peter Weir and Hugh Jackman are known the world over, and aboriginal arts and crafts are just now coming into their rightful place.

Neptune in the eighth indicates the exorbitant taxes that plague this small nation. While other socialist governments have equally high taxation, this levy often kills the desire to excel and better one's economic position. The burden on the government is overwhelming, due to subsidies and the "dole."

The squares to Neptune in the eighth also point to conservative attitudes about sex. Pornography, homosexuality and abortion are topics that are just now being breached. Like most island nations, Australia is traditional, as outside influences have been minimal until recent years. Virgo on this house cusp Indicates the prudish attitude that must Aussie have regarding sexual matters. They would rather do it than talk about it. Remember that Mars is in the fifth house, and despite its retrograde position, indicates a lot of action and energy in matters of this nature.

Venus rules the ninth, as well as the fourth, so Australia is truly a nation of immigrants, just like America. Its conjunction with Saturn, however, has made the Aussie wary of letting in just anybody, and in former years you had to be of European origin, preferably of Anglo-Saxon stock, to get in. While its entry requirements are still among the most stringent, people from southeast Asia are now coming in, provided they have the capital to start a business. Aussies are often distrustful of anyone who doesn't look or act as they do, and this goes for the native Aborigines as well.

Scorpio rules the tenth house, or MC, so sheer survival was the prime consideration of its first settlers. Australia's reputation as a hardy, sun-baked land with unique vegetation and animal life has created an extremely hardy and pioneering spirit. Pluto in the twelfth points to this continent being a former prison colony, as well as the mother country (England) retaining much control over its internal affairs. The queen of England is still the head of state, and her representative, the governor general, still has the power to dismiss any government he chooses. And if you think you can ignore elections, forget it! You're fined if you don't vote, so most elections are held on weekends.

Jupiter ruling the eleventh house points to the most unique aspect of Australian life: mateship. Friendship between males is more than just physical or emotional in nature; it's almost spiritual in concept. A man always remembers to drink and pal around with his buddy when times are good, so that when times got tough, he could always count on his mate for survival and assistance. Relationships between females never reached this level of intimacy, and only Canada (of all English-speaking nations) has a similar concept of male bonding. In America, this mateship between males never caught on, as competition often turned boyhood pals into adversaries. Maybe the geography has something to do with it, for this is a huge land, sparsely populated and ruthless to those who ignore the dictates of Mother Nature. Jupiter on this house makes Aussies optimistic and unaffected, but they do seem to lack a certain mystery or glamour. After all, Sagittarius lays all its cards on the table, so there's no room for deceit. Despite the occasional fracas between friends, however, Aussies don't hold grudges for long, as fire signs are prone to blow up and then forget it.

Saturn ruling the twelfth house, and placed on the ASC accounts for this land's reluctance to acknowledge her convict heritage until recent times. This was something about which to be embarrassed, and definitely not something to discuss in mixed company. Saturn in this house indicates that the one thing which will keep Australia from becoming truly great, and occupying the place she rightfully deserves in the world arena, is the self-critical and inferior image of itself as a second-class nation. Australia is unique, as many tourists are finding out, and has contributed much to modern culture. It should try and expand its own distinct arts and crafts and not try to be a combination of England and America. With this will come more patriotic fervor and a chauvinism that will inhibit Saturn's tendency to sell itself short, due to its own limited ambition combined with a fear and distrust of the future.

Adelaide

Adelaide began life as the first planned city in Australia. Captain William Light laid out this city in a one mile square grid surrounded by parklands on the banks of the Torrens River. Surveyed in mid-January 1937, the first lots were sold two months later. The

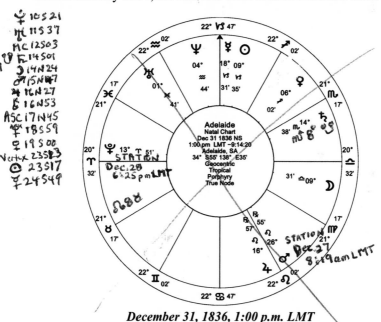

December 31, 1836, 1:00 p.m. LMT
Sources: South Australia State Library and Flinders University Library for the date. Time approximate from statements which imply a time in the early afternoon.

wealthy and idealistic founders wanted only decent, respectable and married people to settle here, in contrast to the convict settlements on the eastern shore. Imbued with a strong work ethic, Adelaide prospered and became the first municipality in the country four years after its founding on August 19, 1840. In 1874, the University was established.

Once known as the "City of Churches," Adelaide today prefers the title of "Festival City." Each even-numbered year since 1960, this city puts on an international festival of the arts which draws tourists from around the world.

Adelaide's Sun in Capricorn points to the conservative lifestyle of the original founders. It's a place where the quality of life is more important than quantity and the preservationist instincts have managed to save most of its famed bluestone houses from the wrecking ball. Capricorn also loves order, so it should come as no surprise to find that Adelaide has some of the most immaculately-groomed gardens in the world. A quiet confidence and aura of competent authority permeates this beautiful city where tradition is important, but not at the expense of progress.

The Moon in Libra sextile Venus and trine Neptune illustrates why Adelaide is an elegant-looking city with refined, cultured and sophisticated tastes. Natives are rather laid-back, but not as much as you'd think due to the Moon's opposition to Pluto and square to the Sun. There's a strong ambition to succeed and a dynamism that's not apparent to the outside world. In recent years, Adelaide has been at the forefront of many liberal and progressive reform movements. It was here that nudists first won their right to sunbathe as they please. Neptune at the MC also indicates the reason why Adelaide is a center for the Australian film industry.

Alice Springs

Alice Springs was founded in 1871 and named for Alice Todd, wife of the Australian postmaster general. It was founded as a telegraphy station to connect Adelaide with Darwin. The town grew slowly and in 1925, its population was only 200 people. The Royal Flying Doctor Service was established here in 1928, one year be-

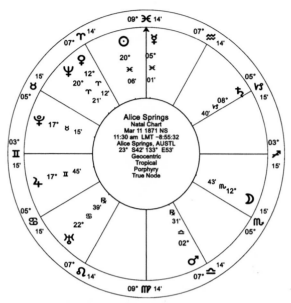

March 11, 1871, 11:30 a.m. LMT
Source: Los Angeles Daily News for the date; time rectified.

fore the railroad arrived from Adelaide (MC sextile Mercury; ASC trine Sun conjunct Uranus square Neptune). Alice Springs is also the base for the School of the Air which allows children on remote sheep stations or in isolated towns to receive an education.

Alice (as the Aussies call it) sits in the middle of Australia, the region they call the "Red Centre" at the base of the MacDonnell ranges. It's more than 1,000 miles to the nearest big city and 275 miles northeast of Ayers Rock, which the Aborigines call Uluru, one of the most spectacular sights in the country. The seven stone buildings on the grounds of the original telegraph station were the first buildings erected in central Australia. One can also view the bungalow for half-caste Aboriginal children.

The people in this part of the country are rugged individualists (Sun sextile Pluto square Jupiter and trine Uranus). They're tough, laconic and used to dealing with this harsh, dry climate (Moon sextile Saturn). This is a region of ranchers, hunters and prospectors who are egalitarian, friendly people with a wicked sense of humor, so typical of most Aussies. Neptune, ruler of the MC, sextile Jupiter and square Uranus, indicates the strong social-consciousness of this city which has brought medical attention and educational opportunities to those in remote places.

Brisbane

Brisbane was founded because the jails in Sydney were becoming too crowded to house the increasing number of twice-convicted felons. John Oxley was sent to explore the region around Moreton Bay in 1823; on September 14, 1824, the convicts landed at Redcliffe. Due to the lack of water, a more suitable site had to be chosen, so Oxley went up the Brisbane River and found water at a bend in the river near the present-day Botanical Gardens. The date was September 28, and on December 2, exactly one year after he discovered the region, the convicts moved here.

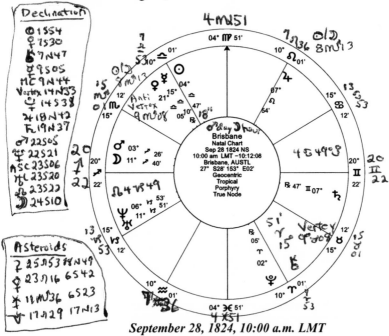

September 28, 1824, 10:00 a.m. LMT
Sources: John Oxley Library for the dates; time approximate.

178

Originally called Edenglaslie, it was anything but paradise due to the violent nature of the criminals. Free settlers were forbidden to come within 50 miles of the place until 1834, when a town was gazetted to honor a former governor of New South Wales. But fortunes declined and the community was abandoned eight years later. With the sale of lots in Sydney in 1843, Brisbane officially came into existence.

During its early years, ships docked at Cleveland on Moreton Bay. A fire burned those wharves in 1854 and Brisbane became the main port of entry. Five years later, Brisbane was chartered as a Municipality on September 7, 1859; three months later it became the capital of the new state of Queensland. In 1864, a fire burned most of the downtown area and the floods of 1869 and 1893 washed away the bridges. The University at St. Lucia was founded in 1909, 11 years before the metropolitan government of Brisbane came into existence. This city played host to the 1982 Commonwealth and Empire Games and put on an Expo in 1988 to honor the bicentennial of Australia.

Brisbane is a tropical city, resplendent with luxuriant foliage due to its high humidity and abundant rainfall. Many homes are built on stilts to protect them from periodic flooding and to cool them during the summer months. The position of Pluto in the fourth square Neptune might account for this anomaly. Like other cities, gardens abound, but unfortunately, they're not as well-tended as they might be. Neptune and Uranus in the 1st indicates the extreme individuality of Brisbane and indifference to outside opinion. Some say it's not a pretty place and many think it needs a good coat of paint. The natives seem to be having too good a time to worry about what their domiciles look like. Brisbane is a place which appears youthful and healthy-looking with well-tanned bodies everywhere.

With Sagittarius rising, Brisbane is expansive, not only in area but in its philosophy. Lax zoning laws have created a rather haphazard look and new developments spring up with little regard for the terrain or tradition. Sun in Libra with its many aspects indicate a people who are unruffled or unhurried and life here progresses at a leisurely pace.

The Moon conjunct Mars might account for the reputation of Queenslanders as being rednecks, arch-conservatives and contemptuous of outside authority. Their strong individualistic streak often takes on violent overtones, for true to their heritage, rebellion is never far beneath the surface. Brisbane is slightly schizophrenic: moralistic and uptight one moment and hedonistic and laid-back the next. The scales of Libra continually swing from one extreme to the other and with four mutable angles, this dualism is accented even further. Despite their reputation as being friendly and hospitable to tourists, some see the natives as really being suspicious of all outsiders. The Sun opposition Pluto or the Moon opposition Saturn might account for this. Brisbane is definitely a hard place to figure out and even harder to get to know well.

Canberra

The Canberra District was formed in 1836, 12 years after the first squatter settlements sprang up. The name means "meeting place" in the Aborigine language. On July 9, 1900, the ACT was agreed to be constitutional assent, but it was eight years before a site was selected, midway between the rival cities of Sydney and Melbourne. A contest for the design of the new capital was held in 1911; two years later, Lord Denman dedicated Canberra. The winner of the design contest was an American, Walter Burley Griffin, of the Frank Lloyd Wright school of architecture in Chicago. He laid out the city in a grand style, reminiscent of Washington or Brasilia, with magnificent vistas, confusing traffic circles and two distinct areas: one parliamentary, the other civic. Parliament moved here from Melbourne on May 9,1927 and in 1946 the Australian National University opened. In 1988, the new Parliament Building was completed on the site originally designated for it by Griffin some 75 years before.

Canberra's Moon, Ascendant and ruler in Taurus indicate the reason this city has such a pastoral feeling. More than four million trees and 10,000 acres of parkland give this city a bucolic aura and government buildings don't overwhelm or intimidate you. The

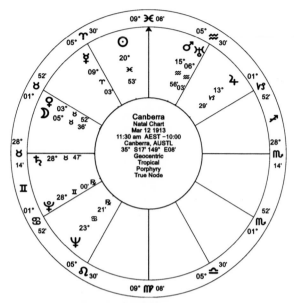

March 12, 1913, 11:30 a.m.
Source: Australian National Archives for the date and time.

Sun in Pisces trine Neptune might indicate why this city is so amorphous, featureless and indistinct. It seems like an artificial place, embryonic and as yet unfinished. Because of the Depression and both World Wars, Canberra has been a long time maturing. But with Saturn rising, nobody's in a hurry down here and for some strange reason, everything is in its proper place. But then it was planned that way, wasn't it?

Mars and Uranus in the ninth house of embassies illustrates why no nation had a consul or ambassador here until the mid-1950s. Note the square of the ninth house ruler, Uranus, to the ruler of the ASC, which is Venus. Devoid of industrial areas, Canberra is a company town, and the business is government. Canberra has little nightlife so most residents entertain at home. Having a bowl chart, Canberra is a very self-contained place, content and satisfied in its isolation both geographically and socially.

181

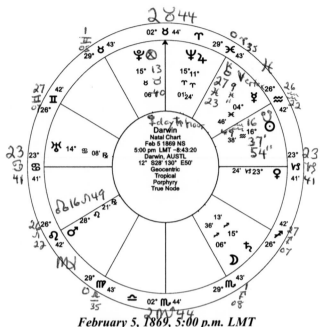

February 5, 1869, 5:00 p.m. LMT
Source: Geoffrey Dean for the date and time.

Darwin

The first settlement of 1864 was abandoned three years after its founding. New settlers arrived in 1869 and called the place Port Darwin, after the famed naturalist. Known alternately as Palmerston until 1911, when the responsibility for the NT passed into the hands of the national government, Darwin was chartered as a city in 1959.

For a city of its size, Darwin has survived its share of disasters. Due to its strategic military location, Darwin was bombed 64 times by the Japanese during 1942. This city has also suffered through many natural catastrophes. The cyclones of 1897 and 1937 were quite severe, but nothing compared to the devastation caused by Tracy on Christmas Day 1974. Winds of 175 mph swept away more than 5,000 structures, killed 66 people and caused 45,000 people to be evacuated. When the residents returned to their city, only 500 buildings were left standing. It was the worst natural calamity ever to hit Australia, and Darwin was declared a disaster area.

But the pioneering spirit of Darwin, shown by its Moon in Sagittarius (and ruler of the ASC) rebuilt the city from the ground up, stronger and sturdier than ever before. The youthful optimism and happy-go-lucky atmosphere of this city is contagious, natives want everyone to have a good time. In years past, Darwin was known as "the beer-drinking capital of the world," possibly because of its isolation. After all, it's more than 2,000 miles to the nearest large city and this town is closer to Asia than it is to Adelaide or Perth.

The Sun in Aquarius shows the natives don't care whether you're rich or poor, black or white, for despite its size, Darwin is probably the most international and cosmopolitan community in Australia. The oriental population is quite large, and even the mayor is Chinese. Darwin's come a long way from the ramshackle town of yesteryear to being the most modern-looking city on the continent. The position of Venus opposition the ASC indicates a place which has a welcome hand to all outsiders, and the Aquarius/Sagittarius lunar placements show it has little sense of false modesty, pride or regard for outdated tradition.

Hobart

Hobart was first explored in 1798 to prevent the French from making further incursions into Van Diemen's Land, as Tasmania was then known. The first settlement in the area was made at what is now Risdon Cove by David Collins on September 7, 1803; but the site proved unsuitable so the community was moved six miles down the Derwent River the following February. Named for the British secretary of state, Hobart was Australia's second penal colony. Mass murderers and other malcontents were sent here so Sydney wouldn't have to deal with them. Thus did Tasmania gain its unsavory reputation. Hobart also was known in its heyday as the roughest port in the world, a place where any vice imaginable could be had for the right price.

Chartered as a municipality in 1842, Hobart became home to

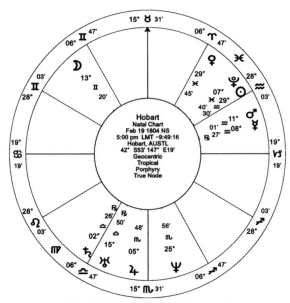

February 19, 1804, 5:00 p.m. LMT
Sources: Tasmanian Archives for the dates. The first settlement in
September was made at 3:00 p.m., according Australian researcher
David Reynolds. The second settlement was made "close to sundown"
according to Hobart Town by Peter Bolger. Chart rectified.

Australia's first synagogue the following year. In 1886, delegates
from the Australian states met here in an attempt to form a Federation; within 15 years they realized their ambition. The beautiful
Tasman Bridge over the Derwent was completed in 1965, and
since Tasmania was the first state to legalize gambling, the first ca-
sino in Australia, at Wrest Point, opened here in 1973.

The worst calamity to hit Hobart occurred February 7, 1967,
when a bush fire spread out of control. Before the flames were contained, 167 square miles were burned and 62 had lost their lives.
Some 2,000 structures were burned to the ground and the damage
was $45 million.

Hobart is a quaint and provincial place that takes pride in the
number of Georgian-style buildings it has managed to preserve.

184

Cancer rising shows the Hobart's dependence on the sea for its livelihood. It's a city of few hassles or long or long commutes as shown by the grand air trine. Hobart is content to keep a low profile for this is a small country town with an idyllic and pastoral feeling, shown by Neptune in the fourth house. This planet also indicates the origins of Hobart as a penal colony. Towering over the city is majestic Mt. Wellington (elev. 4,166 ft.), which is snow-capped throughout much of the year.

Melbourne

Melbourne was founded by John Batman, a free enterpriser from Tasmania. Tired of the limiting environment of that island, he sailed for Port Philip Bay in the fall of 1835. On June 6, 1835 he purchased 100,000 acres of land from the aborigines and paid for it with clothing, food and blankets. The first settlers arrived with

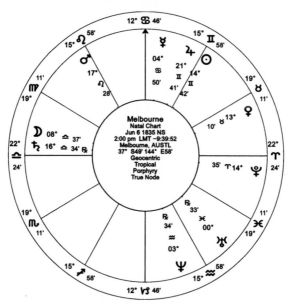

June 6, 1835, 2:00 p.m. LMT
Sources: National Library of Australia for the date. Time from the diary of John Batman which states he purchased the land "in the afternoon." Chart rectified.

185

Fawkner on August 29, and in 1837 lots were sold and the name was formally changed to honor the prime minister of England.

When gold was discovered at Bendigo and Ballarat in 1851, thousands left the city to seek their fortunes elsewhere. During the next three decades, Melbourne experienced its "golden age" as business boomed, the Victorian edifices which line its streets were built and the population tripled. But all the prosperity came to a grinding halt when the Panic of 1889 hit, sending Melbourne's economy into a tailspin. With the creation of Australia in 1901, Melbourne became its de-facto capital, an honor it held until 1927, when Parliament moved to Canberra. This city hosted the Olympics in 1956, and yearly puts on the biggest show in the country when the Melbourne Cup is run in November.

Melbourne is a flat city, laid out in a grid pattern surrounded by numerous parks and gardens. Its streets downtown are 99 feet wide and its business blocks are 660 feet long. The two main thoroughfares are Collins and Bourke; the former is tree-lined and home to many prominent banks and boutiques, and the latter home of Australia's two largest stores, Coles and Myers. Surrounding the center city are the Fitzroy, Carlton and Treasury gardens, and across the lazy Yarra River are the Botanical Gardens and the King's Domain. Metropolitan Melbourne sprawls over 714 square miles from the Dandenongs in the east to Port Philip Bay. It's definitely the Los Angeles of Australia and despite its seaside location, it doesn't have the feeling of a waterfront community.

Melbourne's Sun and Jupiter in Gemini indicates that this city is the heart of Australia's publishing industry. Known as the "Athens of Australia" for its many fine schools, colleges and universities, it's a classy place where class is very important. Note the Moon in Libra conjunct Saturn, the planet of tradition and social status. The ruler of the ASC, however, is Venus and its placement in Taurus indicates why this city is the financial center of the nation. Even though Sydney has more international banks and corporations, Melbourne is where the big bucks flow. Libra rising might also be the reason why Melbourne always tries to present itself as polished, refined and elegant. Saturn close to the Ascendant shows why this city is solid, safe and secure, just like a bank. The conjunction of Saturn to the Moon illustrates why things are pretty serious down here and the reason Melbourne's citizens are private, reserved and take life with much caution. Conservative and rather puritanical, they seem duty-bound and pre-occupied, probably with business. Cancer at the MC shows why Melbourne is a home-oriented city with few tall apartment houses. Residents prefer to entertain by the barbie, despite the numerous fine restaurants and theatres.

Mars in the eleventh house illustrates why Melbourne is so sports-crazy. Its position in the sign of sports and amusements indicates they take their football, cricket, rugby or horse racing very seriously, especially since Mars is sextile Saturn. The intensity with which they yell and shout is shown by Mars' sextile to the Sun and the trine to Pluto. Melbourne might remind you of a time gone by due to its numerous old buildings and its most famous form of transportation, the tram. Cancer at the MC often revels in the past and tries hard to preserve its heritage. Combined with Libra on the ASC it gives a mellow and gracious aura, but don't be deceived, even though Melbourne has been described as a cultured pearl with loads of class but little lustre, this is a dynamic place which in recent years has transformed itself into a very cosmopolitan and sophisticated city. Part of this comes from the many immigrants that have settled here over the past four decades: notably the Greeks who have a community here larger than any outside the city of Athens.

Melbourne is a city of superlatives, shown by its Sun conjunct Jupiter. It has the two largest stores in the country, and the tallest building in the Southern Hemisphere (the Rialto) and its busiest railway station. It also has some of the wealthiest suburbs in the country and its busiest port.

Perth

Perth was founded to insure complete British domination over the continent of Australia. The provincial government in Brisbane sent Captain James Stirling to scout for a site in 1827; two years

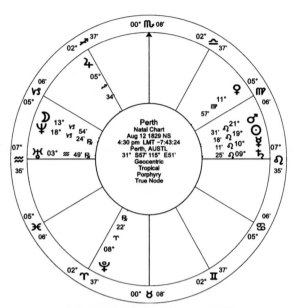

August 12, 1829, 4:30 p.m. LMT
Source: Geoffrey Dean for the date and time.

later the city of Perth was founded and named after a city in Scotland. Located on the beautiful Swan River, its early years were anything but encouraging. The isolation and shortage of workers prompted the city to ask England for convict labor. Created a Municipality in 1856, Perth was the most isolated capital in the world until the completion of the telegraph line in 1877. Its closest city, Adelaide, was 1800 miles east across the forbidding and barren desert. With the discovery of gold at Coolgardie in 1892 and Kalgoorlie the next year, Perth's population quadrupled in 10 years. Perth was finally connected to the rest of Australia when the transcontinental railway was completed in 1917. This city played host to the Commonwealth and Empire games in 1962, and in 1983 it wrested the America's Cup from the U.S. four years later, unfortunately, it had to give it back.

Perth's stellium in Leo and the grand fire trine shows why Perth has the best climate of any capital in Australia. It has the weather Californians just think they have, but without the smog. Perth has

188

been called "Dallas by the Sea" in recent years due to its aggressive, confident, assertive and ambitious people. Uranus conjunct the Ascendant in Aquarius shows us that Perth's eagerness for the future is combined with much progressive thought. But the Moon in Capricorn indicates a people who still revere tradition and are rather conservative, despite their rush for success. The Moon trine Venus in Virgo-points to Perth being a sophisticated and cultured place, but one which doesn't overwhelm or intimidate you. After all, earth signs are the most relaxed of all. That grand fire trine might be the reason why this city revels in all sporting activities, especially maritime events like yacht racing and sunbathing. But then, the MC in Scorpio might indicate the same as well.

When John Glenn flew over this city in 1962 on man's first space flight, Perth turned on every lightbulb in the city to welcome him. Ever since, Perth has been called the "City of Lights." It's a place which has more restaurants and cafes per capita than any city in the country and where you can trek through bushland a few minutes from the downtown area in nearby King's Park. Perth's success might be attributed to the optimism, vigor and vitality of its citizens (again that grand fire trine) which are helpful, friendly and hospitable to the extreme. It's definitely the most typically-Australian city in the nation and one which, in future years, is destined for greatness.

Sydney

Sydney was first discovered by Capt. James Cook in 1770. Botany Bay, his landfall, was deemed unfit for habitation when the First Fleet arrived there on January 18, 1788. Besides, two French ships under La Perouse, had designs on the region. So Captain Arthur Philip sailed 12 miles north into port Jackson, "the finest harbour in the world," to select a more suitable site for settlement. There beside what is now the Circular Quay, the first convicts were sent ashore on the morning of January 26, 1788; later that evening, a toast to the King was made and the city of Sydney was born.

Life was tough in its early years. The climate was unfamiliar,

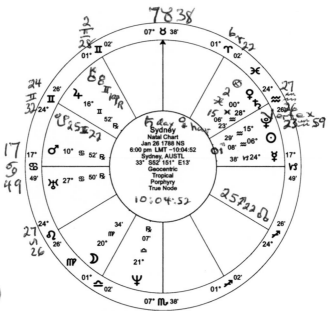

Sydney
Natal Chart
Jan 26 1788 NS
6:00 pm LMT −10:04:52
Sydney, AUSTL
33° S52' 151° E13'
Geocentric
Tropical
Porphyry
True Node

January 26, 1788, 6:00 p.m. LMT

Sources: Allan Johnson uses the time of 7:00 a.m. when the convicts first went ashore. Gwen Stoney prefers a time of 5:30 p.m., while the Sydney Town Hall states the city was founded "about sunset," per the diary of Capt. Philip. Chart rectified.

Declination

```
☽ 15 00
♀ 6 S41
✶
♀ 12 S54
♄ 13 S24
Ψ tx 13 S32
MC 14 N04
☿ 16 N41
☉ 18 S46
♆ 21 N11
ASC 22 N17
♃ 22 N29
⚷ 22 S49
♇ 23 N23
♀ 23 S57
♂ 27 N0S
```

the soil unfriendly to crops brought by the settlers, and the livestock fled into the bush or was eaten by the dingos or Aborigines. Many times, Sydney came close to starvation. Finally after two and a half years of isolation and near famine, a supply ship arrived. But conditions in this "hell on earth" didn't improve dramatically, for drunkenness was rampant and the guards which controlled the convicts were often harsh and cruel in their punishment. To clean up the colony, Captain William Bligh was sent to rectify the situation, but his overhanded tactics provoked a mutiny, and he was driven out of town. His replacement, Lachlan Macquarie, sought to make Sydney a more attractive place by erecting numerous public buildings and laying out new streets and parks. Many of the structures built during his 11-year tenure as governor were designed by Francis Greenway, a former convict. Macquarie estab-

BBC Jan 31, 2007 Sydney in immediate ecological danger
(70 yrs.)

lished a national currency and founded the country's first bank. Sydney was chartered as a city in 1842, 10 years before Sydney University opened its doors. In 1855, the first railway in Australia was completed to nearby Parramatta, the second oldest city in the country.

During the 1890s, Sydney's fortunes began to wane, due to a massive financial depression then gripping the country. Thousands were out of work and banks began to fail. Bankers again thought of forming a Federation to ease foreign scepticism about Australian fiscal stability. Their dream was realized on the first day of this century, January 1, 1901, when this continent became a federation. Despite the fact the proclamation was made by the governor general in Centennial Park, Melbourne was to become the de-facto capital, not Sydney. In 1926, the first leg of the underground railway, or subway, was completed between the massive railway station and the Circular Quay, home base to the many ferries which carried commuters across the harbour.

But the biggest day in Sydney's history occurred on March 19, 1932, when the Harbour Bridge was finally opened to the public. Thousands trekked across its 1,650 foot span to marvel at what was then the longest steel-arch bridge in the world. The "coat hanger" became the prime symbol of this city for more than four decades and helped to spur development of the North Shore. On October 20, 1973, the city's other world-famous symbol, the Opera House was dedicated by the Queen. Financed by a lottery due to escalating construction costs, its radical design by the Danish architect Joern Utzon remains a source of controversy to this day. Somehow, both the bridge and the Opera House blend in quite nicely, both maritime symbols of this city which is wedded to the sea.

Cancer rising points to Sydney being a maritime city, surrounded as it is on three sides by water. No resident is more than five miles from either Botany Bay, the Pacific Ocean or Port Jackson. The magnificent harbour is one of nature's masterpieces containing 36 bays, coves and inlets along its 160 miles of shoreline. Within the metropolitan area are 27 miles of the best beaches on

191

earth. Names like Manly, Coogee and Bondi are famous the world over for their fine surfing, not to mention the handsome lifeguards who protect bathers from sharks or dangerous riptides.

Unlike Melbourne, Sydney is hilly and its streets follow the contours of nature. This city has been described as being "the best address on earth," a place where you can live a champagne life-style on a beer budget. Note the trine of Pluto, ruler of the fourth house, to Jupiter and Neptune giving Sydney not only abundant opportunity but also a romantic aura as well. Pluto ruling the IC might also indicate the numerous architectural styles that abound, all the way from early convict buildings, through Victorian to its present-day circular and octagonal towers. And let's not forget the famed terrace houses in neighborhoods like Paddington, which have recently become the "in" place to live. Fortunately, Pluto loves to restore, and trends are currently underway to preserve much of Sydney's heritage of former years. Despite the architectural hodge-podge, all styles blend harmoniously regardless of their age. Must be due to the grand air trine.

Sydney's Moon in Virgo in the second house points to the entrepreneurial spirit of the city, a place which has abundant variety of consumer goods, many of them in smart-looking shopping arcades. The square of the Moon to Jupiter indicates the desire to take risks and to gamble on future commercial trends. That might explain why Sydney is the most trendy and up-to-date city in the country. Taurus on the MC shows that Sydney is a place which worships money and success, especially with its sextile to Mars and square to the Sun. More foreign corporations and international banks make Sydney their home than any city in Australia. Even though it's not the largest port anymore, it's still the first port of entry for most tourists arriving from foreign countries. Venus, ruler of the MC, conjunct Saturn points to the strong business community which is home to the nation's stock exchange.

Mars rising above the ASC shows that Sydney is a place of abundant energy, drive and vitality. Its pace is quick and rapid, its tempo frenetic. Often bored and impatient, it's constantly trying to surpass even its own expectations. Mars' position in the twelfth house might show the reason why Sydneysiders tend to root for the underdog, especially when the police are involved. Aussies have an inherent distrust of all authority figures due to their convict heritage. Combine this with erratic, independent Uranus in the first house and you have a place that constantly surprises and excites you. The Ascendant falling at the Mars/Uranus midpoint shows why its citizens were described as "the most difficult to govern on earth." Residents love their freedom more than anything else in the world; fortunately most of this violence and rebellion is played out on the sporting fields where they can work off this excessive energy acceptably.

Sydney's Sun and Pluto conjunct in Aquarius makes Sydney the most hedonistic city on the continent. Residents love to party, often into the wee hours of the dawn, for this is an intense and thirsty city that yearns to satisfy its appetites. Like a rough diamond, Sydney glitters and sparkles, especially in the "sin quarter" called King's Cross. No other place in the South Pacific resembles this smaller version of Greenwich Village or Soho. It's a place where delights to tantalize the palate and the flesh can be had most hours of the day. Servicemen on R&R came here from Vietnam to relax and work off steam before they returned to the battlefields. But Sydney takes it all in stride, due to the grand air trine which creates a sophisticated and cosmopolitan atmosphere that is seldom shocked by anything. It's a city which has learned to enjoy life to the fullest.

Jupiter in the eleventh indicates the generally positive reaction that outsiders have towards Sydney. It's a city that makes friends quite easily, and for Australia as well. Natives are among the warmest, most helpful and friendly in the world and they roll out the "red carpet" with genuine affection. Jupiter, as ruler of the sixth house, shows the power the unions have over the workers, due to its square to the Moon in the second house. Many times life seems to come to a standstill due to a work stoppage, but that's a fact of life in all Australia, not just Sydney. Mercury in Capricorn opposite Uranus might show the unique national lingo, called Strine, which many find difficult to comprehend without a dictionary. Note the square of both planets to Neptune in the third house, which rules books. Mercury opposition Uranus also points to the love of free speech and independent thought for which the Australians are so famous.

Life is never dull in Sydney due to its see-saw type of chart. Things are constantly changing and in a continual state of flux. There's a drive and intensity combined with an insatiable curiosity to experience all that nature has laid at their doorstep. Sydney seems to have taken the bull by the horns to create a most unique and fascinating city that ranks among the most beautiful in the world.

Australian Historical Potpourri

Mary Coleman's fine articles on the first Christmas, Captain Cook and Arthur Philip were truly inspiring, not to mention very educational and informative. In an article published in *Horoscope* magazine in November 1979, the chart for Captain James Cook was given with a birth time of 4:15 a.m. As I don't have this article anymore, I don't know whether this was from an entry in the family Bible, parish records, or purely speculative. In any event, that chart gives a MC of 19 Cancer and an ASC of 14 Libra. Planetary positions are the same as in Mary Coleman's article with the exception of the Moon which is late 26 or early 27 degrees of Capricorn.

Two very interesting sidelights about Cook's chart: when you relocate this chart to Botany Bay, the MC becomes 23 Sagittarius and the ASC is 23 Pisces. Using Koch house cusps, Uranus is trine the ASC on the cusp of the ninth and Mars sits at the MC and thus square the ACS as well. Saturn is sextile the MC within three degrees, or maybe even closer if the "birth time" is a few minutes earlier. Seeing how Cook was the person who initiated the exploration and future discovery of the continent, I find it quite fascinating that the two planets which rule those attributes, Mars and Uranus, are in aspect to his angles in Sydney. Ironically, the ruler of the relocated MC, Jupiter, is in the fourth house, so while Captain Philip made the first settlement, Cook literally founded the country.

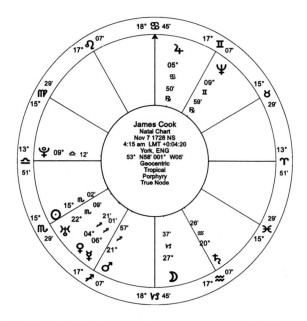

Relocating Cook's chart to the west coast of the island of Hawaii where he was killed in 1779 gives ominous portents of danger. Even though Neptune and Pluto make trines to the relocated MC, the Sun (giver of life and authority) is square that MC within three degrees. The Sun rules the fourth house or end of life, so what we know about Cook in this place is shown vividly in this chart. Aspects to the ASC are terrible: Uranus, ruler of the relocated MC, is opposite the ASC indicating accidents, opposition from "strangers" and when combined with Saturn square the ASC illustrates the necessity to play it "cool" lest one's orders be taken the wrong way. Cook would be blocked in his attempts to control things in this part of the world, and Mars inconjunct the ASC on the eighth house shows his death by stabbing. The relocated progressed ASC at 10 Cancer was square Pluto, another indication of finality and passage into the annals of history.

The First Fleet left Portsmouth, England at 5:00 a.m., May 13, 1787, according *to The Fatal Shore* by Rupert Hughes. Note the placement of the Sun (ruler of the fourth house of settlement) in the twelfth house, which indicates the nature of the people on the

195

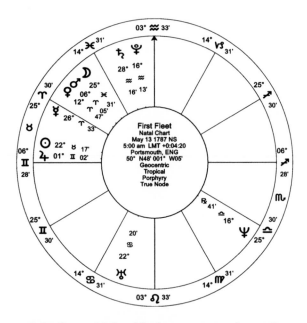

voyage and the future birth of Sydney as a convict settlement. The
Sun square the Saturn/Pluto midpoint at the MC also indicates the
harsh environment these settlers would have to endure once they
landed in Australia, not to mention what they anticipated from authority figures on the long voyage down under. The Moon in Pisces is another indication of imprisonment, but its trine to Uranus
and sextiles to the Sun do show that adverse conditions would
eventually be overcome.

Comparing this chart with Captain Arthur Philip, we note some
very interesting aspects occurring at the time of departure. Saturn
was going over Philip's Moon and would be there again when the
city of Sydney was founded more than eight months later. Saturn
was also trine his Sun, showing good judgment and consideration
for those convicts who were in his trust and care. Mercury had just
gone over Philip's Jupiter so the Captain probably had more "fun"
on his voyage than he originally thought possible. The trip (Mer-
cury/Jupiter) proved quite pleasant considering everything, and
this aspect also indicates good judgement. Philip's natal Mars at
22 Gemini is trine the Saturn/Pluto midpoint of the sailing so with

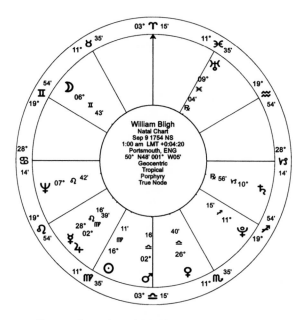

assiduous effort and continual application to erase all signs of possible adversity, the mission would be accomplished if one stuck to the original plan. Neptune in Philip's chart at 3 Cancer opposed his Uranus at 2 Capricorn, both of which made hard aspects (semi-square/sesquare) to that Saturn/Pluto midpoint. So while things went better than planned, it was a journey that Philip probably didn't want to take, but was forced into. The sextile of Pluto to Uranus and the trine to Neptune made the Captain endure and rise above the nature of this mission, one which would give "birth to a nation."

Another person related to Australian history is the infamous Captain William Bligh. Born in Portsmouth, England September 9, 1754 at 1:00 a.m. (per the family Bible) he was the opposite of Captain Philip, a hard and often ruthless sea captain who sparked the most famous mutiny in history. Relocating his chart to Tahiti where he was sent to bring breadfruit back to England, we find that the MC at 5 Scorpio was sextile Jupiter but square Neptune, a sure sign of betrayal and mutiny if I ever saw one. The ASC at 6 Aquarius 30 was trine the Moon but opposing nebulous and deceptive

197

Neptune. Many of his crew, like Fletcher Christian, wanted to remain in Tahihi, and some even married native women. Nearly two decades after the mutiny, Bligh was sent by the Admiralty to become governor of New South Wales where his relocated MC was conjunct Jupiter but square his Moon. Bligh was so unpopular (afflicted Moon) with the convicts and often overstepped his authority (Jupiterian self-righteousness), that he was "run out of town" to be replaced by another Virgo who was also a pain in the ass, just like Bligh.

Fiji

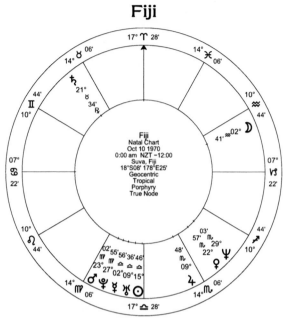

October 10, 1970, 12:00 a.m., Suva
Source: The New York Times

Fiji is composed of 840 islands of which only 105 are inhabited. Lying 1,960 miles northeast of Sydney and 1,100 miles north of New Zealand, most islands are mountainous with tropical forests on the windward sides. The main islands are Vitu Levu and Vanna Levu. Sugar makes up 54 percent of its exports and petroleum accounts for 12 percent.

When Abel Tasman discovered these islands in 1643, they were inhabited by many tribes, some of them cannibalistic. The British arrived in 1804 and began to colonize and 70 years later, Fiji became a British colony after local chiefs relinquished control. Beginning in 1879, indentured workers from India were imported to work the fields as the native Fijians were not used to hard labor. In 1900, Fiji asked to join the New Zealand federation but was subsequently rejected.

Independence from Britain was realized in 1970. A military coup in 1987 erupted when the native Fijians became worried that their country would grant too much representation to the Indians, but calm was restored soon after. Fiji remains a popular stopover for tourists on their route from Hawaii to the countries of New Zealand or Australia.

French Polynesia

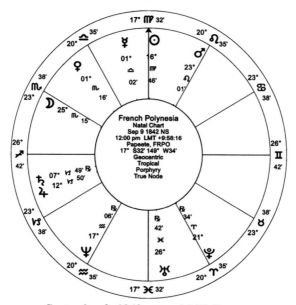

September 9, 1842, noon LMT, Papeete
Source: Department of Tourism and Culture

Captain James Cook visited what was later called the "Society Islands" on his journeys around the South Pacific in 1769. Captain Bligh came here in 1788 in search of breadfruit. His crew fell in love with the islands and its women, so when Bligh insisted on returning home, his crew mutinied and returned to Tahiti, picked up supplies and their women and eventually landed on Pitcairn Island.

This region became a French protectorate in September 1842, and in March 1946, an Overseas Department of France. The French granted partial autonomy in 1977.

French Polynesia lies in the South Pacific midway between South America and Australia and about 4,000 miles southwest of California. It contains 130 islands, including Tahiti, Moorea and Bora Bora, as well as the Marquesas, Gambler, Austral islands and the Tuamoto archipelago.

French Polynesia has 1545 square miles of land and a population of about 250,000, of which half live on Tahiti. About 80 percent of the people are Polynesian and 13 percent are Chinese. The capital is Papeete.

Guam

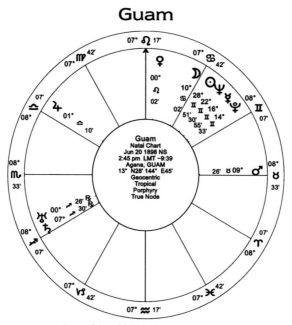

June 20, 1898, 2:45 p.m., Agana
Source: Department of the Interior says between 2:30 and 3:00 p.m.

Spain claimed the island in 1565 and held it until the Spanish-American War in 1898 when Guam was ceded to the United States. Japanese troops occupied the island from December 1941 until the middle of 1944. Due to its strategic location, Guam has become a major military outpost. It's 3,300 miles west of Hawaii and 1,350 miles southeast of Tokyo.

Guam has a coral and limestone plateau in the north, volcanic mountains in the west and very steep cliffs on its eastern shore. Guam is about the size of Chicago in area and has 155,000 residents, many of them in military service.

Kiribati

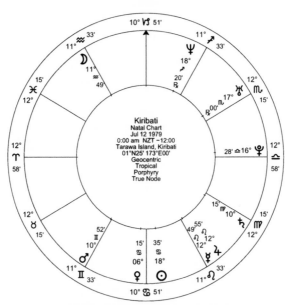

July 12, 1979, 12:00 a.m., Tarawa
Source: San Francisco Chronicle says midnight.

Kiribati is composed of 33 islands, mostly low-lying sandbars no higher than 15 feet above sea level. Copra is the main export.

The first Europeans arrived during the 1830s on what were to become the Gilbert and Ellice Islands. In 1892, these islands were made a British protectorate and in 1937, the Phoenix Islands were annexed. The Japanese seized the region in December 1941 and it was here that the Battle of Tarawa was fought in November 1943. Self-rule came in 1971; four years later, the Ellice Islands seceded and formed the nation of Tuvalu. Independence from Britain came in 1979.

Marshall Islands

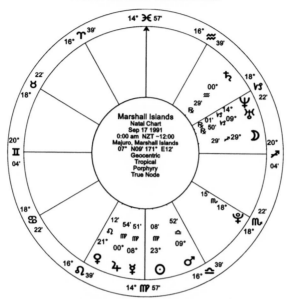

September 17, 1991, 12:00 a.m., Majuro
Source: United Nations

Germany owned these islands beginning in 1899 until the beginning of World War I, when the Japanese took over their administration. After World War II, in 1947, they became part of a United Nations Trust Territory under U.S. administration. During the Cold War, atomic bomb tests were conducted on Bikini and Eniwetok atolls. Independence came in 1991, when these islands joined the United Nations.

The Marshall Islands are a series of 31 atolls in the Pacific Ocean 1,300 miles southeast of Guam and 2,000 miles southwest of Hawaii. Its area of 70 square miles is the size of Washington, DC.

Micronesia

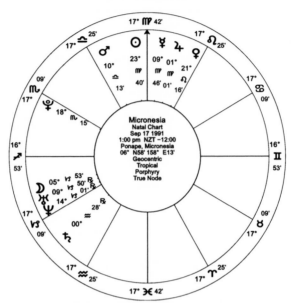

September 17, 1991, 12:00 a.m., Pohnpei
Source: United Nations

Once known as the Caroline Islands, Spain governed them by 1886, and Japan took over after World War I in 1918. Micronesia became part of the U.N. Trust Territory of the Pacific in 1947, and achieved full independence when it joined the U.N. in 1991.

Micronesia lies 500 miles east of the Philippines and its land area is slightly smaller than that of New York City.

Nauru

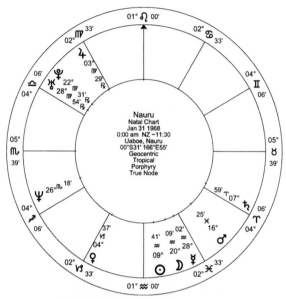

January 31, 1968, 12:00 a.m., Uaboe
Source: The New York Times says midnight.

Nauru is a barren island composed of a plateau surrounded by coral reefs about 2,200 miles northeast of Sydney. Containing only eight square miles, it's the world's smallest nation, with the exception of the Vatican. Phosphates constitute 100 percent of its exports which according to economists should deplete by the early 1990s, leaving the economy in grave danger.

Nauru was discovered by the British in 1798 but was left unsettled for decades thereafter. Germany annexed the island in 1886, but after its defeat in World War I, Nauru came under Australian mandate. Independence was granted in 1968 after the Nauruans voted not to become part of Australia.

New Caledonia

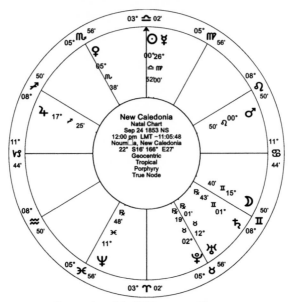

September 24, 1853, noon, Noumea
Source: Department of Tourism.

Captain Cook visited New Caledonia in 1774 on his voyages around the South Pacific. France acquired the region in September 1853 and ran a penal colony here from 1864 until 1897. New Caledonia was made an Overseas Department of France in March 1946. A referendum held in 1987 resulted in the natives choosing to remain part of France rather than seek independence. In 1998, France began to share sovereignty in hopes that complete independence would manifest sometime in the future.

New Caledonia, which includes the Loyalty Islands, is a region of 7,200 square miles about 1,000 miles off the east coast of Australia. Its population of 215,000 is 45 percent Melanesian and 35 percent European. The capital is Noumea.

New Zealand

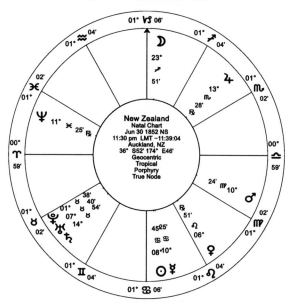

June 30, 1852, 11:39 p.m. LMT, Auckland
Source: Donn Forrest

This island nation was first settled in the 14th century by the Maoris, a Polynesian race of people who probably came here from Hawaii. The region was first explored by Abel Tasman in 1642 and by Capt. James Cook in 1769. Missionaries arrived on the North Island in the early 19th century and on February 6, 1840, the treaty of Waitangi was signed and New Zealand became a British colony. The Maori chieftains handed over large portions of their land to the British overlords, and year by year tensions grew and grew. The first Maori War erupted in 1845 and lasted for three years. The British granted self-rule to this region in 1852 when it was granted a Constitution.

New Zealand's chart is somewhat confusing as to date and time. Years ago when I visited with Donn Forrest in New Zealand, he presented me with a chart for this country showing the Moon at 23 Sagittarius, which is where that luminary would be at the very end of June 30, 1852. Some are of the opinion that the country came into being at the beginning of that day when the Moon was about 10 Sagittarius. The problem was solved a few months ago when a correspondent from New Zealand stated that the British Parliament passed a law granting independence for New Zealand at 12:00 noon GMT. Relocating this chart to Auckland, then the capital, the time becomes 11:39 p. m. LMT with a MC of 1 Capricorn 30.

The second Maori War erupted eight years after New Zealand became a nation and lasted for nearly a decade. New Zealand's progressed MC at this time was sextile Neptune (ruler of the twelfth house of troubles), trine Mars (ruler of war) and opposition Mercury (ruler of the third house of neighbors). The progressed ASC was square Mercury as well as inconjunct Mars. One year after the second Maori War began, a gold rush began on the South Island in 1861 and before long, Dunedin was the wealthiest city in the country. In 1865, the capitol was moved from Auckland to Wellington, as the latter city was more centrally located.

New Zealand has been in the forefront of many progressive activities over the years, being a pioneer (Aries rising) to a great extent. In 1893, it was the first nation to grant women the right to vote, as the progressed MC was square Jupiter (ruler of law) and the progressed ASC was conjunct Uranus (which governs reform) and square Venus (which rules women). Five years later in 1898, New Zealand began the massive welfare state for which it is so famous with the establishment of old-age pensions (progressed ASC trine Mars sextile Mercury and Neptune). By 1907, New Zealand was granted the status of a dominion.

Like Britain before her, New Zealand declared war on Germany in August 1914, and with the Aussies saw massive casualties at Gallipoli the following April. At this time, the progressed ASC was inconjunct the Moon in the ninth house of foreign encounters and ruler of the nation's fourth house of security. During the 1930s, this country suffered along with the rest of the world in a massive economic depression. During the latter part of this decade, New Zealand instituted many reforms, as the U.S. had done

210

before. Social security and unemployment insurance were promulgated as was a minimum-wage law and a 40-hour week. The progressed MC was sesquare Jupiter and semi-square Saturn and the progressed ASC was square both Mars and Neptune, which natally fall into the sixth-twelfth houses of work and health concerns. One year later, under the same basic progressed aspects, New Zealand entered World War II. Shortly before Pearl Harbour was attacked by the Japanese, New Zealand started a program of socialized medicine (progressed MC semi-sextile Pluto, progressed ASC inconjunct Jupiter). New Zealand, along with the U.S. and Australia, formed ANZUS in 1951 as a mutual defense pact (progressed MC inconjunct Mars, progressed ASC semi-square Uranus) and three years later, became a partner in SEATO (progressed MC inconjunct Jupiter, progressed ASC opposition Moon).

The most disturbing event in the nation's recent history came in July 1985, when the Rainbow Warrior, flagship of the Greenpeace organization, was bombed and sunk in Auckland's harbor. At this time the progressed MC was conjunct Saturn and the progressed ASC was inconjunct the Moon, both aspects involving the leader of the country and its reputation as well as foreign or international concerns. Almost immediately, the prime minister pulled out of ANZUS as the U.S. wouldn't agree to permit inspection of certain ships entering New Zealand waters which might be carrying nuclear weapons.

New Zealand also rules over the Cook Islands, Niue and Tokelau, as well as the Ross Dependency in Antarctica. The North Island is extremely volcanic with numerous hot springs and geysers. The South Island is mountainous, home of the Southern Alps whose highest point is Mt. Cook (elev. 12,313 ft.)

New Zealand has 104,455 square miles of territory, about the size of Italy or Colorado. About 70 percent of its three million people are European while about 10 percent are native Maoris.

Auckland

Seven months after Gov. William Hobson signed the treaty of Waitangi, he founded this beautiful city and named it after the Earl

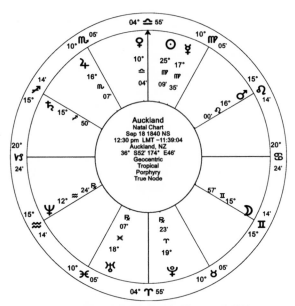

September 18, 1840, 12:30 p.m. LMT
Source: Auckland Public Library says 12:30 p.m.

of Auckland. For its first quarter century, Auckland was the capital of New Zealand, but in 1865, the legislature moved to the more centrally-located city of Wellington. In 1882, its university was founded, one of the finest in the South Pacific. The most disturbing event in New Zealand's history occurred in July 1985, when the Rainbow Warrior, flagship of the Greenpeace organization, was bombed and sunk in Auckland's harbour by French secret service agents. This incident sparked international controversy and eventually led to New Zealand pulling out of ANZUS.

Auckland is the largest city in New Zealand and has the largest Polynesian population of any city on Earth, most of them Maoris who came here six centuries ago. Relations between the pahekas (whites) and the Maoris were relatively peaceful until recent years. But with increasing unemployment, crime has soared and alcoholism has become a national disgrace. Efforts are also being made to assimilate other Pacific islanders into the region, the largest metropolitan area between South America and Australia.

212

Auckland is situated on an isthmus and thus has two harbors: one on the Pacific called Waitemata for large vessels, the other on the Tasman called Manukau for smaller craft. In recent years, the northern suburbs have grown considerably due to the completion of the Harbour Bridge in 1959. Auckland is an attractive place (Venus at the MC) with many spacious parks, some of them lying atop extinct volcanoes like Mt. Eden and One Tree Hill. Mowing the grass in these areas is relatively cheap as sheep do most of the work. Auckland has managed to retain a small town appearance despite its population of one million. Most residents live in wooden bungalows (which withstand the frequent earth tremors) and skyscrapers are rare. Traffic flows with ease and two express-ways wind their way through the city. Auckland is definitely the most cosmopolitan and sophisticated place in New Zealand and unquestionably its business and industrial center.

Auckland's chart is quite complex: all planets fall into either one of the two grand trines, a grand cross or a T-square. The grand fire trine points to Auckland's exuberant nature and dynamism, not to mention its love of sports, especially those which occur on water. The grand air trine illustrates why Auckland has the only international airport in the country and why it's the educational and cultural centre of the nation. The mutable cross might point to the international flavor of the city and potential problems when trying to assimilate various minorities. The fixed T-square indicates the economic importance of Auckland and the need to restructure its fiscal priorities. The above patterns involve a great deal of both optimism and luck combined with great energy and a desire to succeed at any cost. Over one-third of all New Zealanders (or Kiwis if you prefer) live in the region and Auckland is truly a city of super-latives.

Christchurch

Christchurch was the last, and most successful, colonizing project envisioned by Edward Gibbon Wakefield, the English economist who desired to reform the South Pacific. Founded by the Canterbury Assn., an arm of the Anglican church, the first ships landed on December 16, 1850 at nearby Lyttleton; eleven days later when

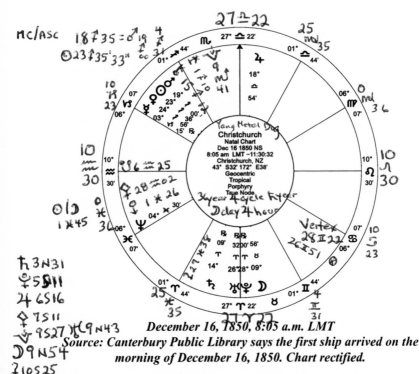

Christchurch
Natal Chart
Dec 16 1850 NS
8:05 am LMT −11:30:32
Christchurch, NZ
43° S32′ 172° E38′
Geocentric
Tropical
Porphyry
True Node

December 16, 1850, 8:05 a.m. LMT
Source: Canterbury Public Library says the first ship arrived on the
morning of December 16, 1850. Chart rectified.

the final ship arrived, the colonists trekked over the Port Hills to
settle this beautiful region they called Canterbury. Unlike other
large cities in the country, the region was flat, so surveyors laid out
wide streets at right angles, unbroken in its monotony only by the
meandering River Avon which runs through the heart of the city.
Being English, they left plenty of room for parks and recreation areas; in fact, over one-eighth of the city is parkland. When Canterbury was chartered as a borough in 1856, its name was changed to
Christchurch to honor the institution which established the community. That same year the massive Anglican Cathedral for which
this city is so famous was begun, and in 1873, Canterbury University was founded, the first of many such institutions which reside
here.

In many respects, Christchurch is a reproduction of a small
English country town, resplendent with beautiful parks and gardens. Note the Moon in Taurus in the fourth house of land, but

214

since Aries occupies the fourth cusp, competition is often fierce among homeowners to win the award for best garden in the city. Christchurch is thus known as the "Garden City," a place often more English than England itself. Schoolboys still wear those cute little outfits with short pants and the architecture is overwhelmingly Gothic or Victorian.

Prior to the outbreak of World War II, Christchurch was largely dependent on agriculture for its survival. Its chief exports were mutton, grains and the tanning of leather. In recent years, however, this city has become the second-largest industrial center in the country, outranked only by Auckland. Christchurch has the largest airport on the South Island and its airbase is the major departure point for all expeditions to the frozen continent of Antarctica.

With Aquarius rising, Christchurch has an aura of culture and refinement, also shown by Venus conjunct the Sun and the Libra MC. Note the stellium in Sagittarius which may account for this city being an educational center as well as the jumping-off point for journeys to the South Pole. Jupiter in the ninth house may also show this fact. With the Sun (ruler of the DSC), Mars (ruler of the fourth) and Venus (ruler of the MC) all in the eleventh house of organizations, we see who founded this city, and in the sign of Sagittarius, religion was obviously involved. The Moon in Taurus shows that despite the fiery nature already shown, Christchurch is a conservative place, and its bowl pattern indicates a rather self-satisfied and contained temperament. Neptune rising may account for the fact that many outsiders miss or badly interpret the apparent serenity and relaxed atmosphere and tend to concentrate on the dynamic activity which pervades this city today.

Dunedin

Dunedin was founded and plotted in Edinburgh by the Presbyterian Church and was to be named New Edinburgh. When the first settlers landed at Port Chalmers in this region called Otago, they decided to call the place after the ancient Celtic name for the Scottish capital. Dunedin was a planned community from the beginning: the heart of the city became known as the Octagon from

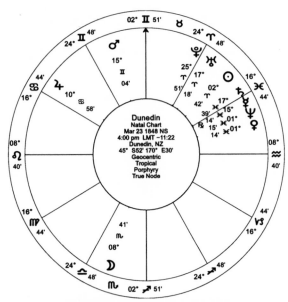

March 23, 1848, 4:00 p.m. LMT
Source: Dunedin Public Library says the first ship landed at Port
Chalmers on the morning of March 23, 1848. Settlers arrived
at present-day Dunedin later that afternoon. Chart rectified.

which all the main streets of the city radiated. Proprietors deemed
it imperative that land prices be kept high so as to discourage other
settlers they felt wouldn't fit into their neatly-planned and
tightly-knit community. Note that a fixed sign rises on the ASC,
often an indication of advance planning, and in the sign of Leo,
this place wanted only the best from the start. Dunedin began life
as a religious centre but when gold was discovered in 1861, piety
went out the window as the town's fortunes grew to immense pro-
portions. With thousands of immigrants arriving each month,
Dunedin soon became the largest city in the country, as well as its
wealthiest. The first institution of higher learning, Otago University, was founded here in 1869, four years after the city was chartered. In 1882, it shipped the first boatload of refrigerated meat to
England.

Dunedin is a gracious and stately-looking city shown by Leo

216

rising and Venus conjunct Neptune in the seventh house. In many ways, however, modern Dunedin is a reminder of its once glorious past, a place to which change comes slowly, shown by the fixed sign ASC and Moon in Scorpio trine Jupiter. Far from the centers of culture or political life, Dunedin has become a backwater of sorts, comfortable and secure in many respects, but always distrustful of change. Mercury retrograde conjunct Saturn might also account for this anomaly, especially since they're both square Mars. Dunedin's preference for the past is also shown by the grand water trine.

Dunedin is to Scotland what Christchurch is to England. It's not all that unusual to see a man wearing kilts in the center city or to hear the nasal strains of the bagpipe off in the distance. Dunedin is also a city of parks and it's famous for its greenbelt which surrounds the city on three sides. But that Moon in Scorpio square the ASC shows the isolation which so pervades this city. If one looks at a world map, one quickly sees that Dunedin is the southernmost large city on Earth: few places on this planet are further south (Patagonia in South America) and the next stop is Antarctica, only a few hours away by plane. This geographical fact plays a large role in the psyche of the Dunedin resident, especially in the winter when the winds howl up from the frozen continent and turn the seas into a tempest. Note also that the Sun/Saturn mid-point is sesquare the ASC, another indication of isolation and loneliness.

Wellington

In September 1839, the New Zealand Company, under the leadership of Edward Gibbon Wakefield, selected the site for the first white settlement in New Zealand. It was decided to name the place after the Duke who defeated Napoleon at Waterloo. The first colonists landed across from the present city at Petone, and sometime later moved their camp to the west side of Port Nicholson. Wellington became the capitol of New Zealand in 1865 due to its central location on a strait between the North and South Island. Its main institution of higher education, Victoria University, was founded n 1897, one of four such colleges in the nation. Over the years Wellington has borne the brunt of many devastating earth-

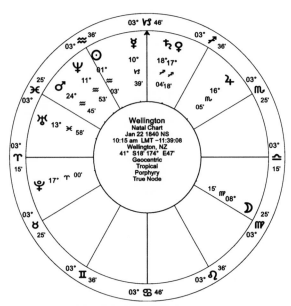

January 22, 1840, 10:15 a.m. LMT
Source: Wellington Public Library and the New Zealand Archives
give the date as January 22, 1840 with no time. Chart rectified.

quakes: those of 1848 and 1942 were particularly severe. The damage would have been more widespread had the homes been constructed of anything but wood. The greatest disaster in New Zealand's history occurred in April 1968, when the ferry steamer, Wahine, capsized and sunk in its harbour, with an extremely high casualty rate.

In many respects Wellington reminds one of San Francisco. After all, both are port cities with steep hills which climb up from the waterfront. Many of the homes are graced with bay windows, and cable cars carry commuters and tourists from the center city to the top of its hills. Only two roads lead out of town, which may explain its relatively low crime rate. But the one thing which most people remember about Wellington is the weather: the wind is often fierce and shakes the very foundations of its buildings, while the rainy squalls come unexpectedly throughout the year. Wellington's most famous structure is the Parliament Building, the largest wooden building on Earth. The annex to the new Parliament Building (called the Beehive) is circular and its architecture in stark contrast to other buildings in the center city.

Despite the fact that Wellington is the political heart of the country, it has managed to retain a small-town image and close ties to nature. Politics don't play as large a role here as they do in other world cities; in fact, most tourists to New Zealand think Auckland is the capital, not Wellington.

Wellington has a bowl chart with the Moon leading the pack and Pluto bringing up the rear, a very intense and often overwhelming characteristic. The Moon's opposition to Uranus might account for its erratic weather and high winds, while Uranus' trine to Jupiter may account for its wetness. Pluto rising shows that Wellington, like most New Zealand cities, lies on an active earthquake fault and is periodically subjected to earth movements. Pluto rising also shows the extensive landfills that have enlarged the center city, thus creating further danger if an earthquake should strike. Wellington's cable cars are shown by Mercury (ruler of transportation) being in the mountainous sign of Capricorn, trine the Moon, ruler of the fourth house.

With Capricorn at the MC, we quickly see that politics is the lifeblood of the city, especially since its ruler is placed in the ninth house of law and conjunct Venus, ruler of the second house of income. Wellington, however, is strictly limited by geography as to how far it may expand. Most of its growth in recent years has been across the harbour in the Hutt Valley which may one day surpass the "mother city" in both area and population. Note that Mars, ruler of the ASC, is placed in a fixed sign and square the planet of expansion, Jupiter. Even the airport is placed in an odd location on an isthmus south of the city, much of it on landfill.

Palau

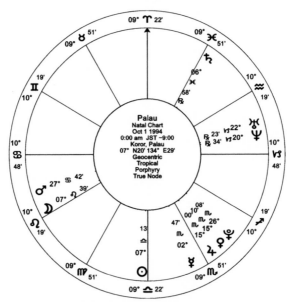

October 1, 1994, 12:00 a.m., Koror
Source: U.S. Dept. of State

Palau became a Spanish territory in 1886, and three years later was sold to Germany. At the beginning of World War I, in 1914, Japan seized the region. In 1947, Palau became part of the U.N. Trust Territory of the Pacific, and independence came in 1994.

Palau lies 530 miles southeast of the Philippines and 720 miles south of Guam. Palau consists of an archipelago of 325 islands, few of them inhabited.

Papua New Guinea

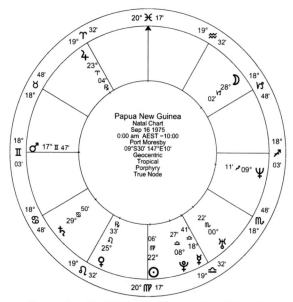

September 16, 1975, 12:00 a.m., Port Moresby
Source: The Times of London says midnight.

This island nation is part of Melanesia and was first settled by the British in 1793. The Dutch took the western half of the island in 1828, which is now part of Indonesia. In 1884, Britain laid claim to the southeast part of New Guinea while the Germans laid claim to the northeast. Australia took the reins in 1906 and gained a mandate in 1921 from the League of Nations.

The Japanese invaded the region in 1942 but were ousted two years later. Independence from Australia was granted in 1975. A rebellion in Bougainville erupted in 1988 and lasted for nine years (progressed ASC inconjunct Moon). A severe drought occurred in 1997 and in July 1998, a tsunami killed more than 300 people.

New Guinea is a land of many tribes, some so isolated they appear to be living in the Stone Age. This is a fertile region for scientists to study evolution and sociology, not to mention that New

Guinea is a treasure trove for archaeologists. This land of five and a half million people is the size of Spain. Lowlands occupy the coastal area while the interior has thick rain forests and high mountains climbing to nearly 15,000 feet.

Port Moresby

The capital, main port and university headquarters ironically has a rather dry climate considering the rest of the country is one of the wettest in the world. During World War II, it was an Allied base and heavily damaged during Japanese air raids.

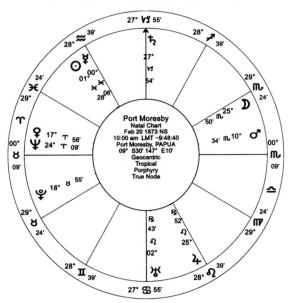

February 20, 1873, 10:00 a.m.
Source: Port Moresby by Ian Stuart.

Samoa

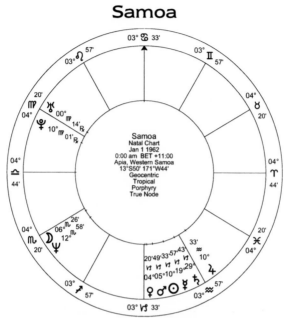

January 1, 1962, 12:00 a.m., Apia
Source: The New York Times.

Samoa is composed of two main islands, Savai and Upolu, and seven lesser ones. Lying 2,200 miles southeast of Hawaii and 800 miles northeast of Fiji, the region is mountainous and volcanic in origin. Cocoa makes up 41 percent of its exports and copra 35 percent.

Samoa was discovered by the Dutch in 1722. Missionaries came to these islands in the early 19th century and converted the natives to Christianity. Samoa became a German colony in 1899, but after Germany's defeat in World War 1, New Zealand took over Samoa's government under a League of Nations Mandate. After World War II, Samoa became a U.N. Trust Territory; independence came in 1962 as Western Samoa, to distinguish it from its American neighbor to the east.

223

Solomon Islands

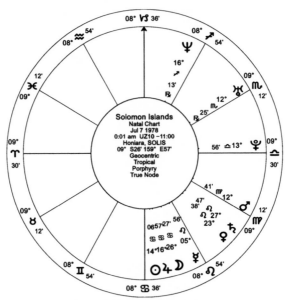

July 7, 1978, 12:01 a.m., Honiara
Source: San Francisco Examiner.

The Solomons are composed of six large islands and many smaller ones. Lying 1,800 miles southwest of Hawaii and 1,100 miles northeast of Sydney, most of the region is mountainous. The highest point is Guadalcanal, which rises to 7,647 feet above sea level. Copra makes up 39 percent of its exports; timber, 27 percent; and fish, 21 percent.

The Solomons were discovered by the Spanish on a voyage from Peru in 1568, but were left uncolonized for the next three centuries. In 1893, the area was made a British Protectorate. During World War II, this region saw many crucial battles (including Guadalcanal) while the Japanese occupied the islands. Independence from Britain came in 1978.

Tonga

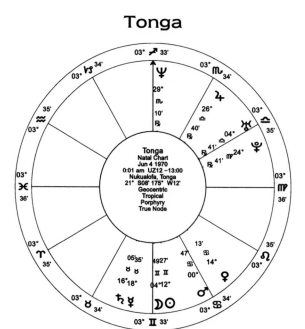

June 4, 1970, 12:00 a.m., Nukualofa
Source: The New York Times for the date;
no time given; midnight presumed.

The Dutch visited these islands in the 17th century and Capt. Cook came in 1773. He was so impressed with his welcome that he named them the "Friendly Islands." Civil wars between the tribes ended in 1845 and Tonga became a British Protectorate in 1900. Seven decades later, Tonga was granted its independence.

In 2001, more than $20 million was lost in a scam due to a Bank of America employee who sold this country questionable financial shares in a company based in the state of Nevada.

Tonga is a monarchy, a region consisting of 170 volcanic and coral islands near the International Dateline in the South Pacific northeast of New Zealand. Only 36 islands are inhabited.

Tuvalu

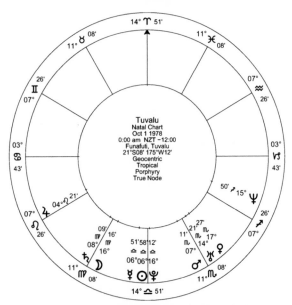

October 1, 1978, 12:00 a.m., Funafuti
Source: Los Angeles Times

Tuvalu is composed of nine main islands, mostly low-lying atolls some 600 miles north of Fiji. Copra is the only export of note.

From 1850 until 1875, Tuvalu saw many of its inhabitants taken as slaves to neighboring islands. With the arrival of British missionaries in 1865, formal European settlement commenced. In 1892, Britain established a Protectorate over the region which was known as the Ellice Islands. In 1975, these islands seceded and formed their own nation, and formal independence came three years later.

Vanuatu

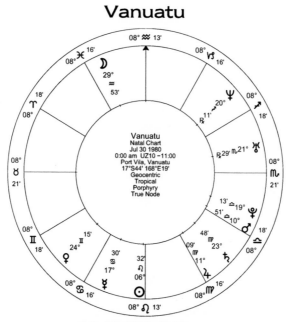

July 30, 1980, 12:00 a.m.
Source: San Francisco Examiner.

Vanuatu is situated in the south Pacific about 1,200 miles north-east of Brisbane. Most of the island is covered by dense forest; a narrow coastal strip contains most of the population.

The Spanish first sighted this island in 1606, but until arrival of the missionaries in the 1820s, European settlement was sparse. During the 1860s, many natives were kidnaped as slaves to work the fields on neighboring islands. In 1906, this island came under joint British and French rule as the Condominium of the New Hebrides. Independence came in 1980 during a recession movement by the island of Espiritu Santo.

Bibliography

General Reference

    Britannica Almanac

    Information Please Almanac

    New York Times Almanac

    TIME Almanac

    World Almanac

    Dunlop Encyclopedia of Facts

    Portable World Factbook by Keith Lye

    Reader's Digest Guide to Places of the World

LIFE World Library

    The Arab World

    China

    Handbook of Nations

    India

    Israel

    Japan

    Southeast Asia

    Turkey

Astrological Books

    Book of World Horoscopes by Nicholas Campion

    Mundane Astrology by Baigent, Campion & Harvey

Printed in the United States
65784LVS00005B/6